of the

Original Lists of Protestant Immigrants

To South Carolina
1763-1773

Compiled By

Janie Revill

CLEARFIELD

Reprinted for
Clearfield Company by
Genealogical Publishing Co.
Baltimore, Maryland
1996, 1999, 2007, 2008

ISBN-13: 978-0-8063-0599-8
ISBN-10: 0-8063-0599-1

Made in the United States of America

Originally published: Columbia, South Carolina, 1939
Reprinted: Genealogical Publishing Co., Inc.
Baltimore, 1968, 1974, 1981
Library of Congress Catalogue Card Number 68-25937

Foreword

The immigrants listed in this volume were protestant refugees from Europe who came to South Carolina on the encouragement of an Act passed by the General Assembly of the Colony on July 25, 1761, called the Bounty Act. A copy of the Act is not available. It is referred to in the published Statutes of South Carolina as follows:

> "AN ACT for repealing an Act passed the seventh day of October, in the year of our Lord one thousand seven hundred and fifty-two, for altering and amending the sixth and seventh paragraphs of the Act commonly called the General Duty Act, and for appropriating and applying three-fifths of the tax appropriated and applyed by the said sixth and seventh paragraphs of the said last mentioned Act as is hereinafter mentioned. (Passed July 25, 1761. The original too much torn to be copied.)"

The explanation or opinion of the Attorney General (page 116 of this volume) shows that it was a broadening of earlier immigration laws, for the special benefit of these religious refugees. Applicants had to have certificates showing that they were protestants and entitled to receive the benefits allowed by the new Bounty Act, which was evidently modified and renewed from time to time.

These immigrants contributed greatly to the religious, social and political development of the Colony, and many of them became soldiers and patriots of the Revolutionary War.

Looking over these lists we find the forbears of some of the most prominent families of the state; and doubtless the forbears of a great many prominent citizens of other states.

In compiling this volume great care has been taken to reproduce the original records (as nearly as is possible) as they were entered in the Council Journals, and therefore no effort has been made to correct spelling, punctuation or other clerical errors. Frequently a family name, or the name of an individual is spelled two or more ways, so that further research and study of the family history would be necessary to determine the correct spelling. In making up the index for this volume a few obvious errors in the spelling of names have been noted in

4

parenthesis so that the names might take their proper alphabetical place.

The records have been compared several times with the original entries, and the work is generally accurate, although the old handwriting proved difficult in a very few instances.

The compiler hopes that this volume will prove of great interest and help to genealogists and students of South Carolina history.

Grateful acknowledgment is due to Miss Elizabeth Fearn Eldridge whose encouragement and financial assistance has made the publication of this work possible.

JANIE REVILL.

Meeting of February 19, 1763.

His Excellency the Governor acquainted the Board that a vessel was arrived in the Port of Charles Town with about seventy persons from Ireland who were come into this Province on the encouragement of Bounty given by an Act of Assembly passed the 25th day of July 1761 That in order no time might be lost in settling those persons in either of the two new Townships lately laid out for Foreign Protestants he had ordered those people to attend with their petitions. His Honor the Lieutenant Governor thereupon observed that in order to distinguish those townships from the others in the Province names should be given them and proposed that the one at Long Cane should be called Boonesborough and the other Belfast The Council agreed in opinion with his Honor and it was Ordered accordingly.

The petitioners were thereupon called in when they were severally sworn to their family right and having produced Certificates of their being Protestants the same were read and approved of.

The following petitions for Warrants of Survey of land &ca were then presented and read VIZ

The Petition of—

In Boonesborough Township.

John Forsith	100 acres and Bounty.		
Andrew Seawright	300 ”	”	”
Richard Brown	100 ”	”	”
David Martin	100 ”	”	”
Mary Martin	100 ”	”	”
James Seawright	100 ”	”	”
James Wason	100 ”	”	”
James McElrath	100 ”	”	”
John Dickson	100 ”	”	”
William McDowell	250 ”	”	”
Michael Dickson	200 ”	”	”
Elizabeth Seawright	100 ”	”	”
David McCrory	100 ”	”	”
Jean Dixon	100 ”	”	”

Robert Thompson	100	"	"	"
Alexander McCracken	100	"	"	"
Henry Templeton	350	"	"	"
Elizabeth Mathews	100	"	"	"
Hugh Kingan	100	"	"	"
Francis Martin	250	"	"	"
James Campbell	100	"	"	"
Matuerin Colvill	100	"	"	"
Samuel Paxton	250	"	"	"
George Seawright	100	"	"	"
James Hathorn	100	"	"	"
John Baxter	200	"	"	"
Hugh Montgomery	100	"	"	"
John Seawright	100	"	"	"
Samuel Seawright	250	"	"	"
Elizabeth Seawright	100	"	"	"
Sarah Martin	100	"	"	"
John Martin	100	"	"	"
Grizel Dixon	100	"	"	"
James Hathorn	300	"	"	"
John McCulloch	100	"	"	"
Jane McCulloch	100	"	"	"
Elizabeth McCulloch	100	"	"	"
Janet McCulloch	100	"	"	"
Jean McCulloch	100	"	"	"
Alexander McCulloch	100	"	"	"
Helen Seawright	100	"	"	"

The Rev'rd John Baxter 500 " " " on proving
Ditto his family right before a grant passes. 600 acres between Broad & Savannah Rivers, notwithstanding a survey made for John Hamilton, deceased.

ORDERED That the Secretary do prepare warrants of survey to the respective petitioners for the land prayed for and that the Clerk of the Council do indorse upon the back of the Certificates produced by the petitioners of their being Protestants, that the said Certificates were read in Council and approved of.

COUNCIL JOURNAL 29, page 24.

It appearing that sundry persons had petitioned for land on family right of children advanced to manhood and entitled to land for themselves, It was thereupon Ordered that no person hereafter applying for Warrants of Survey, be allowd land for any children above the age of fifteen years.

COUNCIL JOURNAL 30, page 14-19.

Meeting of 13th. January 1764.

The Petitions of the following poor protestants lately arrived from Ireland upon the encouragement and Bounty of the Act of the General Assembly of this Province passed the 25th day of July 1761 were presented and read Viz

John Gamble	John Moore
Jane Gamble	James Lindsay
Robert Gamble	John Stephenson
Elizabeth Gamble	John Raphel
Jane Gamble	Mary Browne
Mary Bell	William Browne
William Raphel	Isabel Browne
John Raphel	Agnes Browne
William Brown	George Browne
Elizabeth Brown	Hugh Browne
James Kerrs	Rachel Weir
William Brown	Mary Weir
Hugh McWalter	Jane King
Dorothea Moore	Anne King
Moses Moore	Deborah King
Henry Moore	

The petitioners respectively produced Certificates of their being members of Protestant Congregations & of their good behaviour & receipts in full for their passages therefore humbly pray'd orders on the Public Treasurer for the several Bounties allowed by the aforesaid Act.

ORDER'D That the Certificates be granted to them accordingly.

Read at the same time the following petitions of

William Murdock
Mary Murdock
Anne Murdock
Margaret Campbel
Hester Campbel
Isabella Campbel
John Murdock
John Weir
Henry McNally
John Lavery
Anne Erwine
Elizabeth Miles
Margaret Campbel
Elizabeth Campbel
John Cobran

James Bigham
Patrick Moorland
Robert Fullerton
John Murdock
Elizabeth Murdock
Alexander Murdock
Thomas Miles
William Graham
Mary McComb
James McComb
Sarah Murdock
Jane Bigham
Alexander Hannah
Margaret Bigham

Setting forth that they also were Irish Protestants and lately
arrived on the encouragement of the Bounty therefore humbly
praying the same & it appearing by proper Certificates that they
severally were members of Protestant Congregations in Ireland
and that the owners of the ship in which they came hither had
received consideration for their passages

ORDERED that the Clerk do grant them Certificates as prayed
for.

Read also at the same time the petitions of

James McCollock
John Murdock
Margaret Brenter
David Brenter
Isabella Murdock
Anne Murdock
Francis Murdock
John Murdock
Isabella Murdock
James Sampson
John Browne
Martha Browne
Robert Raphel

James Brenter
Jane Brenter
John Brenter
Isabella Raphel
James Raphel
Mary Raphel
William Little
Anne Little
William Heron
Jane Heron
Robert Heron
Richard King
Jane King

Setting forth that they also were poor Protestants & lately arrived here from Ireland on the encouragement of the bounty & therefore pray'd they might be allowed the same & they also produced Certificates of their being members of a protestant congregation, but it appearing that they severally had not paid for their respective passages

ORDER'D that the Clerk do give their Certificates to Messrs Torrens Greg & Pouag on behalf of the owners of the ship Falls in which ship they were transported hither agreeable to the directions of the said Act.

The acting Commissary attending was called in when his Excellency told him it was the pleasure of the Board that he should endeavor to get Masters for as many of those people as should want them and do everything in his power to prevent their being cheated or imposed upon.

COUNCIL JOURNAL 30, page 20-31
Meeting of 24th January 1764

The following Petitions for Warrants of Survey of lands on the bounty were presented and read

	Acres		Acres
Johnston Rainey	100	David Read	300
William Lindsay	350	Jane Read	100
Jane Read	100	Samuel Read	100
Daniel Gordon	100	St. John Smilley	450
John Gordon	100	Anne Smiley	100
Wm. McElwean	100	John Smiley	100
Hugh McCulloach	100	Wm. Dunwoodie	100
Archibald Strain	100	John Lesslie	150
George Dowdell	100	George Smith	100
Alexander Kennedy	100	Henry Powell	100
John Martin	100	Elizabeth Powell	100
Samuel Young	100	William Levinston	300
Arthur Read	100	Jean Levinston	100
John T ————	250	John Levinston	100
Jane Adair	100	John Greer	150
Hugh Fee	450	Joseph Greer	100
Sarah Fee	100	John Greer, Jun'r	100
Andrew Patterson	250	Andrew Greer	100

	Acres		Acres
Jane Greer	100	Samuel Frizzle	200
Sarah Greer	100	Hannah Cosby	100
William Adams	300	Hugh McConnel	100
Gilbert Lemmon	100	Robert Corrough	100
James Orr	100	Robert McCrachan	400
John Frizzle	100	Mary McCrachan	100

The Petitioners were respectively sworn to their family rights & produced Certificates under the hands of Ministers & Church Wardens of Desenting Ministers & Elders of Congregation in Ireland of their being Protestants & sett forth that they were arrived in this Province upon the enccuragement & bounty allowed by the Act of the General Assembly of this Province pass'd 25th. July 1761 & therefore humbly prayd an Order to the public Treasurer to pay the said Bounties and It appearing that they severally paid for their respective passages

ORDER'D that the Clerk do grant them Certificates to the public Treasurer to pay the said Bounties and that the Secretary do prepare Warrant of Survey to the Surveyor General to cause the land prayd for to be run out to the petitioners in Boonesborough or   Township.

Read at the same time the following Petitions for Warrants of Survey for lands on the Bounty Viz't

	Acres		Acres
James Leslie	100	William McElroy	100
James Barr	300	John King	100
Agnes Barr	100	Jane Lesslie	100
John McConnell	250	William Camlin	100
Margaret McConnell	100	Hugh Duff	100
George McConnell	100	William Law	400
James McConel	100	John Law	100
John Montgomery	100	Thomas McConnel	100

The Petitioners were also respectively sworn to their family rights and produced Certificates of their being members of Protestant Congregations in Ireland from whence they sett forth they were lately arrived upon the encouragement and bounty of the Act of the General Assembly of this Province pass'd the 25th. July 1761 and therefore humbly prayd the same but it appearing that they had not pay'd nor satisfyed the owners for their passages & had covenanted that the Commander of the ship Prince Henry which they came in should receive their respective bounties.

ORDERED that the Clerk do deliver their Certificates to James Egger Commander of the said ship agreeable to the directions of the said Act and that the Secretary do prepare Warrants of Survey to the Surveyor General to run the lands in Boonesborough or Belfast Township agreeable to the prayers of the respective Petitions.

Read at the same time also the following Petitions for Warrants of Survey of lands on the bounty, viz't

	Acres		Acres
Alexander Kennedy	400	John Moore	400
George Watson	400	John Almond	250
Hugh Watson	100	Thomas Gregg	100

The Petitioners were sworn to their family rights and produced Certificates of their being Protestants & likewise humbly pray'd the Bounty and it appearing that they had given considerations for their respective passages

ORDER'D that the Clerk do grant them Certificates as pray'd for & that the Secretary do prepare Warrants of Survey to the Surveyor General to run the lands as pray'd for by their respective Petitions in either of the Townships allotted for them.

Read also at the same time the Petitions of Robert Gibbison and George Gloster setting forth that they also were poor Irish Protestants & lately arrived in this Province upon the encouragement and bounty given by the Act of Assembly & therefore humbly pray'd & Order to the Public Treasurer to pay them the Bounties allowed by the said Act & also an Order to the Secretary to prepare Warrants of Survey for 100 acres of land to each of the Petitioners.

ORDERED that the Clerk do grant them Certificates to the Public Treasurer but that the Order to the Secretary be postpon'd till they were free it appearing that they had severally indented themselves for the term of three years.

Read also at the same time the Petitions of

Margaret Lindsay
Margaret Tisdale
Jane Tisdale
James Tisdale
Margaret Fee
Hugh Fee
Susannah Fee
John Fee
Rachel Fee
Margaret Fee
Mary Fee
Jean Patterson
John Patterson
Jean Patterson
Agnes Read
Margaret Read
Elizabeth Read
Robert Read
Margaret Smiley
Margaret Smiley
Jane Smiley
Elizabeth Smiley
James Smiley
Elizabeth Adams

Robert Smiley
Margery Smiley
Jane Lesslie
Margaret Levinston
Robert Levinston
Margaret Levinston
Mary Levinston
Jane Greer
Sarah Adams
Mary Adams
Elizabeth Adams
Mary Frizzle
Margaret Frizzle
Robert McCrachan
John McCrachan
Agnes McCrachan
Jane McCrachan
James McCrachan
Elizabeth Watson
George Watson
Margaret Watson
Samuel Moore
James Moore

Setting forth that they were Protestants and lately arrived in this Province from Ireland upon the encouragement and bounty of the Act of Assembly therefore humbly prayd an Order to the Public Treasurer to pay it to them & they producing proper Certificates of their being Protestants & also a discharge for their passages ORDERED that the Clerk do grant their Certificates as prayd for by their Petitions.

Read also the Petitions of

Anne Barr
Joseph Barr
Hugh Barr
Jane Barr
Margaret McConnel
Thomas McConnel

Robert McConnel
Rachel McConnel
Jane Law
Robert Law
George Law
William Law

Isiah Law John Almond
Jane Law James Almond
Elizabeth Kennedy James Adair
Robert Kennedy

Setting forth that they also were Irish Protestants & lately arrived on the encouragement of the bounty therefore humbly praying the same may be allow'd them but it appearing that they had not paid for their passages

ORDERED that the Clerk do grant their Certificates to James Egger Commander of the ship they came over in agreeable to the directions of the Act of Assembly.

Read also at the same time the petitions of

Agnes Kennedy Mary Moore
William Kennedy William Moor
Alexander Kennedy John Moor
John Kennedy Thomas Moor
Andrew Watson Catherine Almond
Sarah Watson John Watson

Setting fourth that they also were Irish Protestants & lately arrived in this Province upon the encouragement of the bounty given by the Act of the General Assembly of this Province & therefore humbly prayd the same they also produced proper Certificates of their being Protestants & it appearing that they had severally satisfy'd the owners & Captain of the ship they came over in

ORDER'D that the Clerk do grant them Certificates agreeable the Prayers of their respective Petitions.

Council Journal 30, page 42-45
Meeting of 2 March 1764.

Read the Petitions of the following poor Protestants lately arrived from Germany.

	Acres		Acres
Joseph Kimmel	250	Jacob Inglehard	100
John Ulrick Sutter	100	John Daniel Pitto	100
Andrew John	100	George Henry Lindaner	100
Peter Horlebeck	100	John George Ruppell	100
Frans Gross	100	George Michael Warm	100

14

	Acres		Acres
Peter Elsminger	100	George Matthews	150
George Smith	100	Godfreid Mayer	200
Jacob Rickert	100	Christian Elsminger	300
Conrade Kysell	100	Thomas Schooman	200
Mathew Kenmerling	300		

The Petitioners were respectively sworn to their petitions and also humbly pray'd they might receive the bounty allowed by the Act of the General Assembly passed 25th. July 1761. ORDER that the Secretary do prepare Warrants of Survey for the land prayed for in Belfast Township and the Clerk of the Council do issue Certificates for them to receive the Bounty as prayed for by the petitioners.

Read also the Petitions of Richard Hutchins and Enoch Hainsworth praying for—

Richard Hutchins	100	
Enoch Hainsworth	250	acres of land in Boones borough or Belfast Townships
Alexander Jones	100	

And also the Provision of Bounty.

ORDERED that their Warrants for land be granted and their Certificates to the Treasurer upon their producing proper Certificates of their being protestants.

Read also the following Petitions of—

Eva Catherine Schooman	Philip Jacob Mayer
Barbara Catherina Schooman	Catherine Elsminger, Jun'r
Anna Margaretta Kimmerling	Peter Elsminger
Anna Maria Kimmerling	Christian Elsminger, Jun'r
George Samuel Kimmerling	Margaretta Elsminger
Maria Barbara Kimmerling	Catherine Elsminger
Anna Margaretta Kimmerling	Sophia Mathew
John Jacob Kimmerling	Mary Kimmell
Eva Maria Mayer	John Kimmell

Setting forth that they were poor Protestants lately arrived from Germany upon the Encouragement of the bounty & therefore humbly praying they might be admitted to the same.

ORDERED that the prayers of their Petitions be granted and that the Clerk do issue Certificates to the Public Treasurer to pay to them the bounty allowed by the said Act.

Read also the petitions of—

John Kimmerling   Daniel Poole
Michael Snider   John Peter Dregg
Henry Schell

Setting forth that they also were German Protestants & lately arrived in this Province upon the encouragement of the bounty & therefore humbly praying the same & also tracts of 100 acres of land each but it appearing that they had severally indented themselves for terms of years It is Ordered that the lands and bountys pray'd for by the petitioners be granted when the terms of their respective services shall be expired.

COUNCIL JOURNAL 30, page 53.
Meeting of 6th, March 1764.

The following petitions on the Bounty were also presented and read—

Thomas Higgins	100	Boonesborough or Belfast Township
John Gasser	300	Waters of Savanna River.
Susannah Hopsack	100	Belfast Township
Henry Deares	100	do
Michael Shurrs	100	do
George Sanch	100	do
Elizabeth Foppel	100	do
David Dalgleish	100	do
John Peter Hoynok	100	do
John George Mole	150	do
Charles Mach	100	do

The petitioners were sworn to their petitions & also produced Certificates and prayed to be allowed the Bounty given by the Act of the General Assembly passed in 1761.

ORDERED that the Clerk do issue Certificates accordingly.

Read also the Petitions of—

Dorothy Mole   Margaret Gasser
Mary Gasser, Sen'r   John Gasser
Mary Gasser, Jun'r

Humbly praying that they might be allowed the Bounty given by the Act of Assembly passed in 1761.

ORDERED that the Clerk do issue Certificates to them agreeable to the prayers of their petitions.

COUNCIL JOURNAL 30, page 116-129.
Meeting of 16 April 1764.

His Excellency Communicated to the Board the following Letter from Right Honourable the Lords Commiss'r of Trade and Plantations incloseing an Order from his Majesty in Council relating to the French Protestants Lately arrived here which being read his Excellency desired the Opinion of the Board upon the Subject Matter contained in the said Letter and how the instructions contain'd in the said Letter and Order might be most Effectually carry'd into Execution. The Board observed to his Excellency that as the Season of the Year was now too far advanced for them to set down on Lands to plant provisions against the ensuing crop it wou'd be proper to enquire whether they had means to Subsist themselves 'till the next Crop came about and Messrs Gilbert and Battiton of their Ministers being in Waiting they were call'd in when His Excellency Ask'd them if they were in Circumstances to Support themselves 'till it might be in their Power to get Provisions from their own Culture and if of themselves without assistance they were able to go immediately and set down on such Lands as might be allotted them which they answering in the Negative His Excellency ask'd them what Assistance they would stand in need of and what they had been taught they might expect from this Province to which they Answer'd that they Expected that they were to have a twelve Months Provissions and 20 Shillings Sterling for tools but that through the promisses and insinuation of some People since their Arrival they were entirely Divided upon which his Excellency told them that they might depend upon any Countenance and encouragement the Governor and Council Wou'd show them but he desired them to Assemble them all together and acquaint them that if they expected any favours from the Governor and Council they must pay no regard to what any persons should say to them without their Authority upon which they were directed to withdraw

and his Excellency observed to the Board that as it appear'd
to be his Majesty's intentions that those People should and had
as many opinions as men amongst them settle together shou'd
they once Separate it would be Difficult if not impossible to
Collect them together again and as they had no means of Subsistance among themselves nor cou'd possibly Obtain it if they
Continued in a body he desired the Opinion of the Board if it
wou'd not be a Justifiable Measure in him to Apply the Money
granted by his Majesty out of the quit rents for running out
their Land towards their Subsistance as that Service was Provided for by the Provincial Law the board were of opinion that
his Excellency wou'd be entirely Justified that it woud be very
proper to do so and the Clerk was order'd to serve a Copy of
the said Order on the receiver General of His Majestys Quit
Rents and to demand of him if he was ready to pay the Sums
Necessary for that Service to the Order of the Governor in
Council

Whitehall Nov'r 22'd 1763.

SIR

A Considerable Number of French Protestants inhabitants of
the Southern part of France having latly retired into this Kingdom on Account of their religion and having express'd an in-
clination of settling in some of his Majestys Colonies His Majesty has thought it adviseable that they shou'd be Establish'd
in His Province of South Carolina where from their knowledge
in the Culture of Silk and Vines it is hoped they may be par-
ticularly Usefull to the Colony and to the publick and the
Lords Commiss'rs of his Majestys Treasury having accordingly
enter'd into an Agreement with Mr. Alexander McNutt for the
passage of these People to Charles Town it will be your duty
imediately on their arrival to give them every Countenance
Support and Protection in your Power

Upon this Occasion it falls within our Department to Con-
sider and direct in what Manner these French Protestants may
be Settled with the greatest Convenience to themselves and advantage to the Province and as we conceive that there Ends
will be best answered by their being Placed together in one body,
the Object which We are first to recommend to your Attention is the Laying out a proper Township for them either upon

the river Savanna which is the Situation they seem most to covet or if there are not vacant Lands there within a reasonable distance then upon some other Convenient river and upon such a spot as they shall upon examination find to be most proper for the Object they have in View.

The Number of these People according to the inclosed List is no more than 183 but as there is great probability that if they Succeed in their Undertaking others will follow and join them we think that the Township Allotted them for their settlement Should contain at Least Twenty Thousand Acres of Land to be Laid out in a square Platt one side of which to front the River having a particular Part of it not Exceeding 800 acres reserved in a Convenient Situation for the Site of a Town to consist of about 300 Tenements for Houses and Gardens with Proper reservation for a Common and for a Glebe of three hundred acres for a Minister of the Established Church

As to the particular distribution of the Lands within the Township such distribution must be made to Each family under the regulations and in the proportion prescribed by your instructions as they refer either to the quantity or the Conditions of Cultivation but we think it Necessary to Acquaint you that as the particular situation of these People and their indigent circumstances appears to us to require particular encouragement We have humbly proposed to his Majesty that they shall be exempt from the payment of any Quit Rents for the Space of Ten Years and that the expence of Laying out and Surveying the Lands shall be defray'd out of his Majesty's Revenue of quit rents and we are not without hopes that before the vessel sails We shall be able to send you his Majestys Orders on these points

The advantage which the Province will receive from the requisition of so Large a Body of useful Colonists and the Attention which has always been given by the Legislature there to encourage it Speedy Settlement leaves us no room to doubt that the Council and Assembly will cooperate with you in every measure that can Contribute to the Comfort & Convenience of these People as far as depends upon them and that the Bounty's allow'd by the Act passd in 1761 to each foreign Protestant that arrives in the Province will be pay'd with out delay that of twenty shillings a head for Provissions and tools to the People themselves and that for the expence of Transportation to

such Persons as shall be Authoriz'd to receive it in Consequence
of the engagements which the Treasury have entered into with
Mr. McNutt one Condition of which is that he shall receive
the Bounty in Alleveation of the Expence of the freight

The Reliance We have upon your humanity and zeal for his
Majestys Service makes it Unnecessary to Add anything farther
than that we do most especially recommend this service to your
Attention and to that of the Council and Assembly as his Majesty has been Pleas'd to take these unfortunate People under
his particular Protection and has already extended his Benevo-
lence to them by Supporting them at his Own expence during
their residence here we are

Sir

Your most obedient
humble Servants
Hillsborough

Thomas Boone   Soame Jenyns
Esq'r Governor of   George Rice
South Carolina   Bamber Gascoyne

PS

Under the same Cover with this you will receive his Majestys
Order in Council exempting these French Protestants from the
payment of any Quit Rent for their Lands for ten Years and
you will accordingly insert proper Clauses in their Grants for
that purpose.

Hillsborough.

AT the Court of St. James's
the 18th. of November 1763.

PRESENT

The Kings most Excellent Majesty
in Council

WHEREAS Application has been made to his Majesty at
this Board on behalf of a Number of French Protestants who
have Lately retired into this Kingdom on account of their religion and are desireous of Settling in his Majestys Province
of South Carolina Setting forth the Terms and Conditions upon
which they desire Lands may be granted to them in that Province

AND WHEREAS the Lords Commissioners for Trade and
Plantations and also the Lords of the Committee of Council
to whose Consideration his Majesty thought proper to refer
the said Application have this day made their report thereupon
to his Majesty at the Board Whereby it Appears that the said
Lords Commissioners have taken upon themselves to give proper
directions to his Majesty's Governor for such a distribution of
Lands to these People as shall be expedient for their Settlement
& Accommodation in the manner most Elligible and Convenient
to themselves and most advantageous to the Colonist and the
Publick But in regard to their distress and indigence it might
be adviseable for his Majesty to give Orders for exempting
them from the payment of any Quit rents until the expiration
of Ten Years from the Date of their respective Grants and that
the Expence of Surveying and Laying out their Lands should
be defray'd out of the Quit Rents Ariseing to his Majesty within
that Province His Majesty having taken the same into Consideration was pleas'd with the advice of his Privy Council to
approve of what is above proposed and to order as it is hereby
Order'd that the said French Protestants be exempted for the
payment of any quit rents for the Lands to be granted to them
untill the expiration of Ten Years from the date of their respective grants and that the expence of surveying and Laying out their Lands be defray'd out of the quit rents ariseing
to his Majesty within the Province of South Carolina And
the right Honble the Lords Commissioners of His Majesty Treasury and the Governor or Commander in Cheif of his Majestys
said Province of South Carolina for the time being are to give
the Necessary directions herein, as to them may respectively
appertain.

William Sharpe

Council Journal 30, page 194-195.
Meeting of 28th. May 1764.

His Honour the Lieutenant Governor acquainted the Board
that Mr. Boutiton and the Deputies from the French Colonists
to view the Land proper for them to settle upon had return'd
and that Patrick Calhoun had come to Town with them and
brought Three Platts of different Tracts of Land which his

Honour produced to the Board and the French Men being attending were call'd in and ask'd if they had seen any Lands that wou'd be proper for their Purposes to which they reply'd that they had been over a good deal of Land some of which was bad some indifferent and some very good and they then explain'd on the Platts the Situation that they Esteemed the Best and most Proper for them but desired before they made final choise that they might Consult the Colony and they were then directed to withdraw.

COUNCIL JOURNAL 30, page 139-143.
Meeting of 18th. April 1764.

The French Protestants attending were called in: took the oath of allegiance & also swore to the truth of their several petitions praying for Land and Bounty which were then presented and read viz:

	Acres		Acres
Jean Louis Gibert	200	Anne Beraud Brien Ayne	150
Anne Curreau Bouchonneau		Mathew Beraud	250
	150	Daniel Louis Jennerett	100
Pierre Hile Belot	100	Piere Boutiton	100
Jean Bell Hay	200	Piere Boutiton	100
Joseph Bouchelon	150	Francis Bayle	100
Jean Baptiste Petit	150	Piere Leoron	100
Jean Roger	150	Louis Villerett	100
Piere Regnew	150	Nicholas Basson	100
Piere Nicola	150	Antoine Billaw	100
Colas Bodazean	300	Marie Magdale Belott	100
Jean Bellott	250	Jean Autmeri	100
Jean Baptiste D'Laune	350	Marie Rogers	100
Jean Baptiste Gautier	250	Jeremiah Rogor	100
Jean Lafay	200	Piere Roger	100
Marie Faresteau Gabau	150	Daniel Due	100
Abram Jacob	250	Theodore Gay	100
Piere Roque Mou Ayne	250	Jean Don	100
Jacque Labruese	250	Jean Cartau	100
Jacques Langell	300	Jean Pierre Bellier	100
Jean Fresille	300	Piere Garrineau	100
Jaque Boutiton	150	Nicholas Bouchonneau	100

	Acres		Acres
Charles Bouchonneau	100	Marie Thomas	100
Anthoine Farrasteau	100	Susanna Latou	100
Andrew Guilhibaw	100	Anne Latou	100
Francois Prouvillae	100	Martha Amnien	100
Jean Anthony	100	Jean Dupuy	100
Jean Bouchillon	100	Pierre Langell	100
Marie Bayle	100	Jacque Langell	100
Cecilly Bayle	100	Jacob Baylard	100
Pierre Bayle	100	Pierre Moragne	100
Jean Priolot	100	Matthiew Testall	100
Jean Brian	100	Mathew Beraud	100
Pierre Cluzzeau	100	Jean Beraud de Conton	100
Jean Audibert	100	Pierre Pieron	100
Susanna Roquemore	100	Anny William	100
Pierre Roquemore, Jeun	100	Phillip Berd	100
Pierre Rocquemore Anne	100	Pierre Sudze	100
Piere Rolland	100	Joseph Labbe	100
Francois Gros	100	Jacque Vallae	100
Estienne Thomas	100	Jean Scervante	100

COUNCIL JOURNAL 30, page 144-146.
Meeting of 24th. April 1764.

His Excellency desired the Board to take into their Consideration, what was to be done for the French Protestants, as the Commons house of Assembly was again at an end without doing any business. Fort Lyttleton was proposed as a place where they might reside till their Lands were run out, and Lieutenant Outerbridge who was Lately quarter'd there being sent for was examined whether he apprehended the Land was fertill enough near the Fort & in a Condition to expect some Provissions this Summer and whether there was Lodging room enough for the whole Colony, both which he answer'd in the affirmative and then withdrew; The Board agreed that it would be a Spot proper for their residence and it was order'd that the Clerk do call on the Receiver General and acquaint him that the Expence of runing out the Lands for the Poor French Protestants would amount to £2461:16ᵉ:10 Currency and to require of him if he will be ready to pay it as it may be wanted to the

Order of the Governor In Council and that the Clerk do Lay a State of the Expence for subsisting them for four Months at the following allowance pr Month before the Board.

1 lb flour 1 quart Indian Corn each pr Diem
1 Steer pr Week among the whole
1 Corn Mill Salt &ca.

The Commissary Generals Account with the Township fund was laid before the Board and it being suggested that there was several Demands now due from the said fund. His Excellency sign'd an Order for £1000..—..— on the Public Treasurer out of the Balance in his Hands due the said Fund

The Board proposed as the only expedient applying the Sum Granted by his Majesty out of the Quit rents to defray the expence of running out their Lands towards their Subsistance.

Council Journal 30, page 147.
Meeting of 26th. April 1764.

The Clerk agreeable to the Order of the Last Board day Laid before the Board a State of the Expence to be incurred for the Maintenance of the Poor French Protestants for four months which is as follows

4000 Wt. of flour @ £4/10 pr Cwt. is	£180
400 Bush'ls of Corn @ 12/6 pr Bush'l	250
16 Steers @ £12:10 each	200
20 Bushels of Salt @ 10/	10
A Corn Mill	15
A Canoe	30
Hooks & Lines	20
Hire of 4 horses & a guide for the Deputies to view the Land they choose to pitch upon	280
Charges on Transporting the Colony to Fort Lyttleton	232:10
	£1217:10

And also the following Schetch of rules for their provisional Subsistance.

As the Colony has arrived too Late in this Season for to set down and Plant provisions for their Subsistance the ensuing Winter on the Lands that are to be finally allotted to them the Governor and Council thinks it proper that they should go into the County to Fort Lyttleton which is near the Sea Coast where there is ground already clear'd to plant some Corn Potatoes Pumkins Peas &ca. which will help to contribute towards their Subsistance and where their is sufficient Lodging room for the whole Colony For 4 months by which time the new Crops will come in.

They will be supply'd at the following Rates

    1 lb. flour 1 quart of Indian Corn per Diem ea
    4 Steers per Month among the Whole
    1 Corn Mill Salt &ca will be provided

As the Country where they are to reside is near the sea and abounds with river they may take Large Quantities of fish to enable them to do which they will be provided with a Canoe Hooks & Lines and also twine to make a Nett and it is recommended to them to be industrious in this as it will greatly contribute to their Comfortable Subsistance

In the Distribution of Provisions the strictest Oconomy is to be obseved and as they will probably have more than they can consume it is recommended to them to make a store of what they can spare as it will inable them to set down on their New Settlements with greater Ease and Comfort

They will be transported in Vessells at the Kings Charge to the Place they are at present Destined to go

They are desired to pitch upon three of their Number who are best acquainted with the sort of Land proper for raising the Manufactories they intend to go upon who will be profided with Horses and a guide and as soon as the Land is pitched upon will be survey'd to them accordingly to the Different Proportions allotted them by Virtue of their Family Rights.

As the Success of the Colony will greatly depend on their Living together and keeping up a good Understanding among themselves, it is strongly recommended to them that they suffer no Divission or Quarrels to break in upon them or separate them, as it will be productive of every bad Consequence, since by such Conduct they will be deprived of the Means of rendering the mutual Helps and Assistance to each other which they will be able to do while they Continue in a Collected Body and the Governor expressly declares to them, they must no longer expect any Encouragement or Contenance from him than they Continue to Live with Peace and Harmony together

In Case of private Disputes they are recommended to apply to Mr. De La Gay a Frenchman who resides near the Spot they are to go to, and who will conduct them to the civil Magistrates to whose care and Protection they will be recommended to compromise their Differences and do justice to all partys agreeable to the Law of the Land

As their Number is so considerable it is recommended to them as very Proper to have a constant Guard of six Men to stand Centinals, 2 at a Time Night and Day as well for the better securing their Property as the Prevention of any Fatal Accidents by Fire

They are desired to choose five of their Number, who are to have the Direction of their Domestick Oconomy in Distributing their Provisions overseeing their Works and to preserve Peace and good Order among them, but in Case they cannot perswade the Parties differing to agree they must apply to the civil Magestrate and if he cannot take Cognizance of it recourse must be had to the Governor and Council

If they continue together with Peace and Cordiallity 'till they are settled upon the Land to be allotted them they will receive every Encouragement and Countenance that the Gov'r can shew them, and Industry will not fail to raise them to Ease and Affluence, but should they once seperate they will find as they must no Longer depend upon any Publick Assistance nor can receive mutual help from each other that they have taken wrong measures and will probably fall into States of Indegence and Misery

And several of the French People being in waiting they were call'd in & it was read and explain'd to them

And then his Excellency sign'd an Order on the Receiver General of the quit rents to pay to the Commissary General £200 Proclamation towards the Defraying the Charge of Transporting and subsisting them to at Fort Lyttleton.

COUNCIL JOURNAL 80, page 170-173.
Meeting of 3rd. May 1764.

Read the following Petitions on the Bounty—

Acres

Pierre Michael Pierson 100 and Bounty ⎫

John Smith   200   Do   allowed by the

Jannet Smith   for the Bounty   Act passed in 1761.

Eleanor Smith   Do ⎭

ORDERED that the prayers of their Petitions be Granted
and the Clerk do issue Certificates to the Public Treasurer to
pay them the several bountys allowed by the said Act.

COUNCIL JOURNAL 30, page 209-214.
Meeting of 5th. June 1764.

Read the following Petitions for Warrants of
Survey ....On the Bounty—

Goody Clements   100 ⎫

John Rhoderin   100

Simon Frazier   100 ⎬ In Belfast Township.

Thomas Gown   100

John Gregg   100 ⎭

: The Petitioners also produced Certificates of their good behaviour and pray'd to be admitted to the Bounty allowed by the
Act of the General Assembly passed in 1761 which was accordingly allowed them.

Acres

John Little   150   at the Congarees

Daniel Fenshaw	100	
Patrick McGuire	100	Boonesborough Township.
James Henry Butler	100	these Petitioners pray'd as
Thomas Dingwell	100	before and the Bounty was
Ross McMahon	100	allowed them
Robert McNaight	100	
Agnes Frick	100	

Anna Eva Kendar 100

Barbara Eytinger 100

Heronimus Geer 100

On the waters of Santee

—Saludy River or the waters thereof.

COUNCIL JOURNAL 30, page 225.

Meeting of 14th. June 1764.

Read the petition and Certificate of James Reyley praying for 350 acres of land in Boonesborough Township and also the Bounty allowed by the Act passed in 1761.

Ordered that the prayers of his petition be granted.

Read also the Petitions and Certificates of Mary Reyley, Samuel Reyley, John Reyley, David Reyley, setting forth that they were protestants & lately arrived in this Province on the Encouragement of the Bounty given by the Act of the General Assembly passed 25th. July 1761, and therefore humbly praying that they might be allowed the same.

ORDERED that the prayers of their several petitions be granted.

COUNCIL JOURNAL 30, page 241-245.

Meeting of 3rd. of July 1764.

Read the following Petitions for Warrants of Survey ....On the Bounty:

Patrick Dunlop	100	
Rob't Davison	100	
David Crees	100	In Boonesborough or
George Rounds	100	Belfast Township
Samuel Wells	100	
Jos. McElheany	150	
James Ramage	150	On Pee Dee River
John George Ganter	100	On Saludy River
Postian Fonses	150	Dorchester Parish

The Petitioners produced proper Certificates of their being Protestants and humbly prayed to be allowed the Bounty granted by the Act of the General Assembly of this Province passed 25th. July 1761.

ORDERED that the said Bounty be allowed them.

COUNCIL JOURNAL 30, page 249-250.
Meeting of 4th. July 1764.

Read the Petition and Certificates of Sarah Ramage Dorothy Urwin Mary Holiday and Sarah Holiday praying for the Bounty allowed by the Act of the General Assembly of 1761 which was granted them accordingly

Read the Petitions of

	Acres	
Henry Urwin	250	In Boonesborough and
Wm. Holiday	200	Belfast Townships
and the Bounty		

ORDER'D that the Prayers of their Petitions be granted them on their entering into Security to the Public Treasurer to produce proper Certificates in Twelve months from this date.

COUNCIL JOURNAL 30, page 259-261.

Meeting of 13 July 1764.

His Honor the Lieut Governor inform'd the Board that the Head of the French Colonists were to set out on Monday next and that the rest of the Colony wou'd soon follow—and Communicated the following Letter which he thought proper for their regulation and a Copy of which regulation he had sent to Mr Calhoun

SIR

You will receive this by the hand of Mr Roger whom I have app'd a Justice of the Peace to decide differences amongst his countrymen of the Colony and given him Simpsons Justice for his guide in cases of difficulty I have directed him to Confer with some discreat Justice in his Neighbourhood in w^h I rely on your good Character to Assist him according to the best of your Knowledge.

I have given Commiss'n of Capt. to Mr. Due Lieut to Mr. Leoron and Ensign to LeViollette that they may do militia Dutys by themselves and not be liable to misunderstandings with officers who cannot give their Order in a Language at present understood by the Colonists

Some Persons with the Name of Commissary must be chosen by them to take care of and Issue their Provissions once a Week at the rate of 1 lb of wheat flour or 1 quart of Indian Corn a day to each Person

You are to furnish them with 3 months Provisions 1/2 flour & half Indian Corn and I will pay you for it every 3 or six months on your producing a Certificate from Mr. Roger of the delivery thereof and provided I have no cause to find fault with the Price which from my present good opinion of your honesty I hope I shall have no room to do And as I have thrown many benefits into your hands in running their Lands I expect you will do every friendly office for them which besides dischargeing your own Concience by so doing will most sertainly if this Colony should thrive and become very Populous as it will if properly encouraged now promote the value of all the Neighbouring Lands these being men who fly from the religious oppressions in france will be followed by many also the account of enjoying Civil and religious Liberty here

Upon there arrival as I hope you have executed my orders in purchaseing the Lands at the Fork of Long Canes at a reasonable rate you are to set out 800 acres in a square for the Town in the following Manner.

The Town to be Laid in 200 1/2 acre Lotts and all Numbered is ....100 acres

For the Fort Church Yard Parsonage in Town Market Place which will serve as a Parade Public Mill ea 1/2 acre and Land taken up in the Streets will be about 25

For a Common out of which must be reserved to the Government a right of Granting 50 acres to make 100 more Lotts if the increasing of the Town renders it necessary 200

For a Glebe for a Minister of the Church of England..300

To be disposed of in 4 acres Lotts for the Cultivating their vines and olives in the Infancy of this Colony which they are very solicitous to obtain while they are afraid to go to their Plantations these Garden Lotts to be Numbered 175

Total 800

There shou'd be three or four roads Leading from the Town Laid out two or three miles whose Courses being known may prevent the Tracts being Cut in two by the roads to be run afterwards.

All this should be Carefully Laid down on a paper and one Copy left with Mr. Roger for the Use of the Colony and the other returned to me and Lodged in Council Office.

When the Colony is Arrived and set to Work you are to run out the Limits of the whole Township taking in at Least 20,000 Acres but 6 or 8000 Acres more may be taking in if so much good Land can be found keeping the form as near a Square as the General goodness of the Land will admit but not to take in a Large body of barran Land in order to keep to a square

The Lines are to be marked Plain and 2 or 3 of the Elder men may accompany you in surveying that they may be better acquainted with the boundary's of their Township.

They are to build Houses for their Town and a Fort in it not Less than 120 feet square of Palisades for their Common Security to which they may retire on any alarm and not abandon the Settlement in which must be kept their store of Provision arms and ammunition

As soon as these Works are almost finished you are to begin Surveying their Lands according to their family Warrants to prevent Tumult and Confusion in this Work you are to begin running according to your Surveying Instructions In the st Place for Mr. Rogers the Justice 2nd. Mr. Boutiton the Minister 3'd Capt Due 4th Lieut Lioron 5th Ensign Le Violette unless he gives his right to his Father 6th The Commissary of Provissions 7 the Physician 8th Schoolmaster if any after these the remainder are to take their turn by Ballan to be determined in presence of the 5 first named who are to serve as a Council to the Colony in all difficulty case and take Order therein till the Matter can be referred to the Gov'r in Council for their further direction

You are to purchase immediately a good Cow and Calf for every 5 Persons taking Care that they are branded and marked in such a Manner to prevent dispites with any English Neighbours if you buy them at reasonable Prices I will pay for them on produceing a Certificate from Mr. Roger of their being delivered let their Horses also be branded

A Public mill ought to be Erected as soon as Conveniently Cou'd they may by hunting (not looseing time from their Work) in Company of some rangers procure some Venison this will save their money which their Eating of Beef will Consume too fast

I have now Capt Calhoun wrote you a long letter to give you very Particular instructions in order that this Settlement be Conducted with most expedition Convenience harmony and success I rely on your Punctual Attention thereto when your business is done your are to Come to town and report to me your Proceedings therein with a Platt of the Township and Town and a State of the Colony

I am
Sir
Your very Hble Servant—

COUNCIL JOURNAL 30, page 267.
Meeting of 18th. July 1764.

Read the Petitions of

George Grierson for 200) acres of land on the waters of
Jane Grierson for 100 } the Catawba River
and the Bounty allowed by the Act of the General Assembly
passed the 25th. July 1761.

ORDERED that the Prayer of their Petitions be granted.

Read also the Petitions of Catherine Greirson, Sen'r and
Catherine Greirson, Jun'r pray'g for the Bounty allowed by
the said Act.

ORDERED that their Petitions be granted.

COUNCIL JOURNAL 30, page 286-291.
Meeting of 7 August 1764.

Read the following petitions for Warrants of Survey
..............On the Bounty:

	Acres
Patrick Plaine	100
John Davidson	100
Kennith McKenzie	100
Robert Walker	150

In Boonesborough of Belfast
Township.

Henry Smith	100	
Christopher Footel	100	The Petitioners produced proper
Patrick Carmichall	100	Certificates of their being
John Summers	100	Protestants and pray'd the
Francis Brae	100	Bounty which was allowed.
Peter Martin	100	

Charles Galhager   100   Certificate for Bounty to be granted when he produces a proper Certificate of his being a protestant.

George Henhogs   100 ⎫

Hans Odom Fontes   100 ⎬ In or near Purysburgh Township

    ⎭

Peter Martin   100   Boonesborough or Belfast Township.

COUNCIL JOURNAL 30, page 316-322.
Meeting of 2nd. October 1764.

Read the Petition of—

Timothy Craine   100 acres ⎫

    ⎬ In Boonesborough or

Samuel Beldman   100   " ⎭ Belfast Township

James Simpson   150   "   on Savannah River
and the Bounty allowed by the Act of the General Assembly passed the 25th July 1761

ORDERED that their Petitions be severally rejected, it appearing that they were not within nor entitled to the bounty given by the said Act.

COUNCIL JOURNAL 30, page 348.
Meeting of 9th. November 1764.

Read the Petition of—

Margaret Sheriff
John Herlebeck
George Peterson
John Gourley
John Petty Rew
Samuel Aydon

Setting forth that they were Protestants lately arrived & praying for 100 acres of land in Boonesborough or Belfast & the Bounty allowed by the Act of the General Assembly passed the 25th. day of July, 1761.

His Honor the Lieutenant Governor informed them that the said Act was expired and it was ordered that there petitions be rejected, but they were told they might have land on their Family Rights paying their fees, which they declined accepting of.

COUNCIL JOURNAL 30, page 388-391.

Meeting of 24 Dec. 1764.

His Honor the Lieutenant Gowernor informed the Board that he had this morning sent an Express to Patrick Calhoun to desire him to proceed directly to the spott where the Dutch people were to be settled & there to build a large log House to shield them on their arrival from the inclemency of the Weather that he expected Waggons in Town in about ten days to carry up there baggage That he should write to Mr. Fairchild the Deputy Surveyor to proceed with them and survey the lands and settle them on them immediately that they might avail themselves of the earliest opportunity in raising their hutts and planting there crops and several of them attending they were called in when they were sworn to their Petitions and also took the oath of allegiance & then the following petitioners praying Warrants of Survey were presented and read, viz.

Names	Acres	Names	Acres
Abram Frick	250	George Webber, Sen'r	350
Christian Zang	350	Peter Knabb	150
Philip Zemmerman	350	Fred'k Webber	100
George Fred. Elbeck	200	Hendrick Adolph	300
Magdelen Erlbeck	100	Christopher Hamel	150
Carl Weitman	150	Philip Gradnahl	150
Martin Blomhurt	100	Peter Straub	300
Melchor Fudgell	100	Peter Mehl	200
Martin Plieser	100	Phil Pet. Knabb	100
Michael Pleiser	100	Ann Eliz'h Straub	100
Johannes Seiles	100	Johannes Zanss	150
Erdmund Spudd	100	Margaret Derin	100
Wilherm Boneth	100	Margaret Knab	100
Ann Eliz'h Keiss	100	George Dorn	150
George Weber, Jun'r	200	Phil Keiss	300
Michael Leman	100	Maria Eliz'h Knab	100

	Acres		Acres
Michael Keiss	250	Conrad Muck	100
Maria Cath'a Keiss	100	Johannes Flick	450
Henry Schwartz	300	Frederick Zemmerman	300
George Weelhelm	250	Balker Merk	400
George Schillkneth	350	Anna Catherina Weissen	250
Peter Dorst	150	Adam Heme	400
Henrick Rubert	203	Peter Herne	100
Eliz'th Rubert	100	Maria Eva Straub	100
Johan Nich'l Kimber	200	Henrick Straum	150
Andrew Marks	200	Rachel Derins	100
Valentine Keen	350	ORDERED that the Secretary
Johan Adam Buren	300	do prepare Warrants of Sur-
Johannes Zwilling	250	vey agreeable to the prayers of
George Feltman	300	the respective petitions.

COUNCIL JOURNAL 32, pages 412-427
Meeting of 31st. January 1765.

Read the petition of William Woodrop and Andrew Cathcart of Charles Town, merchants, setting forth that they were Agents for the Committee in London for the relief of the poor German protestants lately arrived in this Province in the ship Dragon, Capt. Hammett, and Union, Capt. Smith, and praying that the Bounty of Five Pounds Sterling for each of the following persons might be paid to them to be by them applyed to the use and directions of the said Committee of German protestants, the said Committee having defrayed the expence of the said German protestants' passages to this Province.

	Ages		Ages
Hans Gall	42	Agnes Franklin	14
Herman Smith	30	Johan Cheves	13
Johan Grubert	30	Regina Seveitzenn	12
Christian Gallin	36	Johan Mathew Metzer	32
Madelina Zemferin	38	Johan Geo. Shoemaker	41
Sus'a Regina Seveitzerin	25	Frank Witten	52
Margaret Gallin	16	Michael Greissen Trein	32
Ann Eva Ansman	16	Jacob Shoeber	29
George Michael Gall	14	George Michael Kennern	27
Ann Maria Hagin	14	Philip Jacob Sheildkneckter	50

	Ages		Ages
Jacob Walts	50	Albreckt Beckman	64
Ann Margarta Braunen	23	John Fred. Beckman	23
Maria Elizabeth Rousen	40	Eva Eliz'h Albrickten	47
Catherine Schieldkneightin	48	Anna Barbara Beckman	44
Catherine Walts	45	Susannah Beckman	21
Maria Miswillering	18	Josias Beckman	16
Andrew Rouson	18	Maria Dorothea Beckman	19
Henry Gast	18	Maria Beckman	12
Henrick Sanbrick	17	Johannes Flick	40
Henrick Cam	17	Peter Bradshern	40
John Freidweismiller	14	Henrick Snark	45
Anna Maria Rouson	14	Christopher Hamell	29
Rudolph Rouson	12	Abram. Freitz	32
Maria Elizabeth		Sabina Flicken	43
Schieldknightin	13	Ann Marg'ta Bradsherer	33
John Hen Ferdinand	32	Anna Schwartz	40
David Stanold	42	Ana Eliz'h Hanon	60
Johan Jacob Messersmith	31	Ana Catherina Freitzen	34
John Clame	35	Eva Flicken	16
Johan Geo: Pericot	36	Eliz. Schwartzin	16
George Sheuer	40	Maria Hamelin	19
Nicholas Glasser	34	Henrietta Flicken	13
Andreas Kentzen	27	Barbara Flicken	13
Johans Boshert	30	Margaretta Swartzin	14
Philip Wm. Bundles	24	Peter Dorst	39
Catherine Ferdinand	46	Philip Zimmerman	36
Apoliona Stanford	42	Johannes Welling	40
Eva Cath. Messersmith	24	George Webber, Sen'r	52
Eliz'h Clem	27	George Wilhelm	40
Maria Glasserin	28	Christian Zang	40
Catherine Kentzem	24	Anna Maria Dorsts	29
Barbara Keiterin	40	Apolonia Zimmerman	37
John George Walts	20	Maria Zwilling	30
Catherine Sheurin	20	Catherine Webber	46
Martha Waltzin	12	Maria Wilhelm	40
Anna Cara Edelmansin	14	Juliana Zang	32
Jacob Stanold	14	Barbara Webber	16
George Fred. Pericot	14	Susanna Webber	19
Eliz'h Keuterin	12	Christian Wilhelm	12

	Ages		Ages
Peter Strum	66	Barbara Marskin	27
Belshazer Merk	46	Anna Eliz'th Dorren	36
Valentine Khunn	46	Marg't Zebberdeen	22
Maria Strum	50	Elizabeth Feltman	32
Eliz'h Merk	38	Rachel Duerin	17
Anna Maria Khunn	33	Eliz'h Keiss	19
Catherina Knabin	53	Peter Kenn	16
Eliz'h Knabin	91	Peter Knabb	50
Elizabeth Strum	20	Philip Peter Knabb	24
Maria Eva Strum	16	Henrick Adolph	38
Susannah Merk	18	Nicholas Keiss	46
Conrad Merk	16	George Schieldknight	36
Maria Barbara Strum	1	Peter Mehl	39
Johan: Jacob Strum	12	Maria Adolph	26
Locenty Merk	14	Eva Keiss	45
Rosina Merk	12	Cath'a Schieldknight	28
Barbara Khunn	12	Cath'a Schwartz	35
Adam Boner	40	Anna Maria Mehl	30
Philip Keiss	42	Maria Knabb	19
Frederick Zimmerman	36	Catherine Keiss	16
Frederick Erlbeck	30	Marg't Schieldknight	14
Michael Zinman	40	Anna Schwartz	14
Catherine Bruser	39	Henry Rupert	42
Maria Keiss	37	Nicholas Rumpe	34
Margaret Zimmerman	36	Henrick Strum	24
Sophia Erlbeck	27	Philip Grateworth	27
Elizabeth Zinman	40	Carl Weidman	38
Eva Keiss	12	George Webber, Junior	25
Johannes Zants	27	Adam Ken	39
Andrew Merks	31	Catherine Rumpe	39
George Dorsen	30	Eliz'h Strum	23
Martin Blumenhart	24	Anna Gratewohl	26
Melchor Flugell	33	Eva Weidman	34
Johannes Taylor	25	Barbara Webber	23
Michael Plieffer	25	Anna Eliz'h Kenn	38
John Baker	23	Elizabeth Rubert	16
Wm. Bonnett	30	Frederick Webber	16
George Feltman	36	Christopher Rupert	12
Margaretta Durin	49	Eliz'h Kenn	12
Margaretta Sank	21		

ORDERED that the prayers of the petitioners be granted, and
that the public Treasurer do pay unto the hands of the said
William Woodrup and Andrew Cathcart the sum of five pounds
sterling for each of the said German protestants to be applyed
for the use of the Committee and German protestants agreeable to the said Resolution and Act.

Read also the petition of the said Wm. Woodrop and Andrew
Cathcart Setting forth that the following German protestants
had arrived in the said ships from London and are since deceased and praying that the Bounty of four pounds and two
pounds sterling, according to the respective ages of the said
German protestants might be paid into their hands to be applyed by them for the use and according to the directions of
the said Committee who had also defrayed the expense of the
passages of the said German protestants into this Province.

	Ages		Ages
Johan George Weidness	65	Anna Blemenskin	40
Christopher Ursman	53	Cathereine Bosherting	39
Christian Zwertzer	60	Wm. Anderson	50
Barnard Franck	52	Sophia Weismellers	45
Johan Shewer	54	Johanes Anderson	49
Bartho. Sleifer	26	Anna Catherine Walk	21
Christian Frank	40	Barbara Sherrer	16
Anna Cath. Andrew Willet	75	Jacob Sweitzer	18
Anna Cath. Willet	34	Maria Blumentskin	16
Maria Phillipia Swietzer	36	Andreas Unsman	17
Margaret Shoemaker	54	Catherine Weidners	11
Magdalene Shewrer	39	Jacob Frank	12
Anna Maria Weidners	45	Urban Sherrer	8
Maria Shieldknight	22	Conrad Bercott	6
Johannes Shoemaker	14	Ann Barbara Carles	8
John Conrad Walk	15	Eva Albright	6
Christian Weidner	15	Mathew Kunold	5
Martin Walk	7	Anna Albright	5
Christopher Elbright	11	Anthony Weith	3
Michael Braun	2	Johans Kunold	3
Christian Franklin	3	Johan Braun	3
Johannes Haag	60	Martin Pleiser	25
Anna Maria Buckhart	38		

ORDERED that the prayers of their petitions be granted, and that the public Treasurer do pay unto the hands of the said Wm. Woodrop & Andrew Cathcart the sums of four pounds and two pounds sterling according to the respective ages of the said German protestants to be applied by them as the said Committee may appoint or direct agreeable to the said resolution and Act and prayers of the petitions

Read also the petitions of the said Wm. Woodrop and Andrew Cathcart setting forth the following German protestants under the age of twelve and above the age of two years now arrived in the ships from London and praying that the Bounty of Three Pounds Sterling for each of them might be paid into their hands to be applied for the use according to the directions of the said Committee who had also defrayed the expence of the Passage of the said German protestants into this province.

	Ages		Ages
Hans Adam Keiss	9	Henry Webber	11
Anna Keiss	6	Johannes Zimmerman	9
Hans Schieldknight	6	Anna Zimmerman	9
Madela Schwartz	6	George Zwilling	10
Catherine Adolphin	5	Johannes Zwilling	9
Elizabeth Adolphin	3	John Peter Wilhelm	10
Adam Schieldknight	4	John Peter Zang	9
Lorank Weiss	3	Peter Zimmerman	4
Moria Mehl	4	Johan Webber	3
Fred'k Rupert	9	John Jacob Zang	7
Margaret Hen	8	Anna Maria Merk	9
Nicholas Hen	6	George Khunn	8
John Fred'k Hen	3	Christian Zang	4
Barbara Hen	2	John Zang	3
George Frick	11	Maria Strum	5
Elizabeth Frick	8	Henrick Merck	4
Adam Schwarcher	6	Jacob Merk	2
Maria Frick	6	John Henry Khunn	4
Anna Freitz	10	Angelica Bauern	11
Peter Freitz	8	Carles Bauern	8
Margaret Freitz	3	Maria Keiss	7
Peter Bradsherer	2	Anna Zimmerman	7
Adalalia Zimmerman	11	Eva Zetheman	8

	Ages		Ages
Maria Bauern	2	Johannes Pitzen	8
Gothel Keiss	4	Henry Switzer	4
George Zimmerman	2	Urier Sherin	5
Maria Erlbeck	2	Margaret Hagen	5
Henry Zehman	5	Catherine Zeiserin	4
Dorotha Zehman	3	Christian Shoemaker	11
Johans Doran	10	Adrian Whitten	6
Anna Merksin	2	Maria Sheildknight	10
Eliz'h Feltman	3	Rosina Shieldknight	6
Anna Catherina Feltman	5	Marcus Stanhold	8
Dorothea Hagen	11	Christian Glasserin	10
George Ausman	11	Maria Kuterin	10
Martin Gall	8	Henry Boshert	6
Joseph Weidner	10	Anna Maria Boshert	10
Andrew Blumerstock	8	Mathew Albright	9
Anna Sherin	8	Maria Beckman	2
Catherine Ausman	7	Catherine Boshart	9
George Sevitzer	10	Albrick Beckman	8
Margaret Sevitzer	8	Jacob Waltz	3
Christian Pitzen	10	Christian Beckman	6

ORDERED that the prayers of their petitions be granted
& that the public Treasurer do pay unto the hands of the said
Wm. Woodrop & And'w Cathcart the sum of Three Pounds
Sterling for each of them to be applied to the use of the Committee and German protestants agreeable to the said resolution
and Act.

Council Journal 32, page 455.
Meeting of 27th. February 1765.

The following Petitions of the German protestants addressed
to His Honor the Lieutenant Governor Setting forth that they
were safely arrived in the ship Dragon Captain Hammet and
Planters Adventure Captain Lonley from London and humbly
prayed to have Warrants of Survey for the following tracts
in Londonborough Township free of charge were presented and
read VIZ

	Acres		Acres
George Michael Gall	100	Barbara Micheal	100
Hans Gall	150	Peter Khunn	200
Marg't Gallin	100	Paul Shawrer	150
Magdelen Zeuserin	150	Martin Wees	100
Herman Smith	100	Thomas Hoslin	100
Anna Maria Hagen	100	John Bert	100
Johan Grubert	100	Andreas Rouson	100
Agnes Francklin	100	Michael Grein Frein	100
Anna Eva Asmin	100	Henry Gart	100
Susanna Regina Seveitzerin		Henrick Ham	100
	300	Jacob Sauber	100
Johan Mathew Metzer	100	George Michael Kennern	100
Franck Witten	150	Philip Jacob Schieldknight	300
Johan George Shoemaker	150	Jacob Walt	250
Ana Marg'ta Branen	100	Johan Jacob Walts	100
Maria Weismellerin	100	Johan Fred'k Ferdinand	150
Johan Fred'k Wadmeller	100	Anna Caradassin Edel-	
Maria Eliz'h Rouson	200	mansin	100
Albright Beckman	350	David Hanold	250
Johan Mich'l Beckman	100	Johan Jacob Hermer-	
Susannah Beckman	100	smith	150
John Fred'k Beckman	100	John Clem	150
Maria Dorothea Beckman	100	Johan George Pericott	100
Nichol Gream	150	George Fred'k Pericott	100
Michal Shaffer	150	George Shauer	150
George Hornersin	150	Nichol Glasser	200
Peter Keibber	200	Andreas Zentzen	150
Michael Sherer	100	Barbara Kentarin	200
Bernard Buckells	200	Johans Boshert	250
Johan Langwalt	200	Philip Wm. Rundler	100
Valentine Michael	100	Eva Elizabeth Albrighten	150

ORDERED that the Secretary do prepare Warrants of Survey for the above Tracts of Land in Londonborough Township and that the restive officers do charge their fees to the Receiver General of the Quit Rents agreeable to his Majesties most gracious instruction.

ORDERED that the prayers of their petitions be granted & that the Secretary do prepare Warrants of Survey accordingly and that the charges of surveying and granting their

Lands be paid out of the quit rents agreeable to his Majesties most gracious direction & order.

His Honor informed the Board in regard that more German protestants might possibly hereafter arrive he it would be expedient to lay out a larger quantity of land than was now wanted and that he thought it would be proper to lay out about 25,000 acres which the Board advised his Honor to give directions for accordingly.

COUNCIL JOURNAL 32 page 468.

Meeting of 5th. March 1765.

The following petitions on the Bounty were presented and read

	Acres		Acres
Peter Foss	100	Michael Warm	100
Mannerwell Waggener	100	Peter Dinner	250
Henry Timble	100	Jacob Record	100
John Bishop	300	Jacob Williamer	100
Edward Welch	100	Stephen Files	100

In Boonesborough or Belfast Township.

The Petitioners also prayed to be allowed the bounty given by the Act of the General Assembly passed the 25th. of July 1761 and all except Stephen Files and John Smith who had before received the Bounty produced proper Certificates of their being protestants and good behaviour.

ORDERED that the Clerk do grant them Certificates according to the prayers of their Petitions.

ORDERED that a Certificate be granted to the said Stephen Files on his producing the Certificate required by the Act.

Read also the Petitions and Certificates of

Anne Bishop, Sen'r	Christiana Dinner
Mary Bishop	Fred'k Dinner
Ann Bishop, Jun'r	Juliana Dinner

Setting forth that they were protestants lately arrived in this province on the encouragement of and hunbly praying to be allowed the Bounty given by the Act of the General Assembly passed the 25 of July 1761

ORDERED that the Clerk do grant them Certificates accordingly.

COUNCIL JOURNAL 32, page 566-570.

Meeting of 2nd. July 1765.

Read the following Petitions on the Bounty—
Nicholas Fitting
      100 acres in Londonborough Township & Bounty.
Finley Campbell
      100 ” in Belfast   &   do
Anna Eva Schooman
      150 ” in Amelia or Orangeburg &   do

Read also the Petitions of John Woodin Thomas Woodin Elizabeth Woodin Rebecca Woodin & Ann Oxenham setting forth that they were Protestants Lately arrived in this Province on the encouragement of the Bounty and humbly praying to be allowed the same.

ORDERED that the Clerk do grant them Certificates to the Public Treasurer & that the Secretary do prepare Warrants of Survey agreeable to the prayers of their respective petitions.

(Page 576) The following Petitions for the Bounty allowed by the Act of the General Assembly of this Province passed the 25th July 1761 were presented & read VIZ

      Thomas Woodin
      John Woodin
      Elizabeth Woodin
      Rebecca Woodin
      Ann Oxenham

ORDERED that the Secretary do prepare Warrants of Survey the Surveyor Gen'l certify the platt & the Public Treasurer do pay the Bounty agreeable to the directions of the said Act provided the Petitioners for the Bounty do give security to the public Treasurer to repay the same in twelve months if they do not within that time produce the proper Certificates required by the said Act.

Council Journal 32, page 608
Meeting of 10th. September 1765.

Read the petitions and certificates of

	Age	
Mary Pattison	37	years
Thomas Pattison	15	"
William Pattison	13	"
Marg't Pattison	10	"
Ann Pattison	7	"
John Pattison, Jun'r	3	"
Mary Pattison	3	"

Setting forth that they were descended from and also were themselves Protestants and of good Behaviour and were lately arrived in this province from Ireland on the encouragement and Bounty allowed by the Act of the General Assembly passed the 25th day of July 1761 and therefore humbly praying Orders for the same.

ORDERED that the Clerk do issue Certificates to them agreeable to the Prayers of their Petitions.

Council Journal 32, page 612.
Meeting of 18th. Sept. 1765.

Read the Petitions of—

> Henry Davies
> Dorothy Davies
> Henry Davies
> Mary Wingate

Setting forth that they were protestants arrived in this Province from Great Britain on the encouragement and bounty given by the Act of the General Assembly of this Province passed the 25th. July 1761 and therefore praying for the same.

ORDERED that the Clerk do grant them Certificates to Public Treasurer to pay the same.

Council Journal 32, page 623.
Meeting of 2nd. Oct. 1765.

The following Petitions set forth that the Petitioners were Protestants and arrived in the Province on the encourage-

ment of the Bounty given by this Province of the Act of the
General Assembly passed the 25th July 1761 were presented
and read and the Public Treasurer ordered to pay them the
Bounty allowed by the said Act.

Helen Fellows
Mary Fellows
Anne Fellows
Eliz'th Fellows
Abram Fellows
Helen Fellows

COUNCIL JOURNAL 32, page 653.
Meeting of 5th. Nov. 1765.

Read the Petitions of the following persons setting forth
that they were foreign protestants lately arrived in this province
on the encouragement of the Bounty given by this Province
by Act passed by the General Assembly the 25th. July 1761 &
therefore humbly pray the same.

John Brunet	100	
John Gurly	100	In Boonesborough or Belfast Township.
Mary Brunet	100	

ORDERED that the Clerk do issue Certificates to the Public Treasurer to pay them the Bounty agreeable to the directions
of the said Act.

Read the petition of Paul Miller setting forth that he arrived
in this Province from Germany 12 years ago on the Encouragement of the Bounty given by the Act of the General Assembly
of this Province and therefore humbly prayed the same.

ORDERED that the Commissary Gen'l do pay him the same
accordingly.

The following petitions on the Bounty were read but the
petitioners not producing the proper Certificates Ordered that
they be severally rejected, viz

James Wyley
Henry Cardwell
Catherine Brown
Thomas Dalton.

Read the petition of John Sailes setting forth that he had intermarried with Anna Evashcoosnan a German protestant lately arrived in this province who had never any Warrant of Survey or grant of land in this province for herself & two children & therefore pray'd for a Warrant on the Bounty for 150 acres in Amelia Township.

ORDERED that the Secretary do prepare a Warrant of Survey accordingly.

Council Journal 32, page 662.
Meeting of 16th. November 1765.

Read the Petition of George Adamson setting forth that he & his wife were foreign Protestants & had lately arrived in this Province on the Encouragement of the Bounty given by the Act of the General Assembly passed on 25 July 1761 & therefore prayd an Order to the Surveyor General for 150 acres of vacant Land and an Order on the Treasurer for the Bounty aforesaid.

ORDERED that the Secretary do prepare a Warrant of Survey accordingly & that the Clerk do issue his Certificate to the Public Treasurer to pay him the Bounty agreeable to the directions of the said Act.

Council Journal 32, pages 668-671
Meeting December 4, 1765.

The following Petitions of some poor protestants lately arrived into this Province from Great Britain and Belfast in Ireland praying for Warrants of Survey for lands & the Bounty given by the Act of the General Assembly passed the 25th day of July 1761 were presented and read—

	Ages	Acres
Wm. Crosley	36	600
John McCue	33	200
James Webb	49	350
Thomas Graham	20	150
Roger Agnew	20	100
Thos. Beathy	16	100
Joseph Walker	21	100

Samuel Fisher	19	100
Joseph Moore	33	350
John Lesslie	38	400
Thomas Lesslie	40	400
Patrick Barr	19	100
John Wallace	24	100
John Thomson	23	100
Joseph Gregg	22	100
William Hannah	21	100
Anthony Duffield	23	100
Daniel Perry	20	100
Hugh Simpson	18	100
Mary Hunter	32	100

In Boonesborough or Belfast Township & producing the required certificates of their being protestants & of their good behaviour & also receipts for their Passages.

ORDERED that the Secretary do prepare Warrants of survey and that the Clerk do grant them certificates to the public Treasurer to pay them the Bounty agreeable to the directions of the said Act.

Read also the following petitions for Warrants of survey and the Bounty—

	Ages	Acres
John Walker	44	350
Agnes Walker	18	100
Henry Furguson	20	100
John Maxwell	32	350
William Beatty	46	100
Joseph Turner	18	100
James Gray	35	150

In Boonesborough or Belfast Township.

The Petitioners produced proper certificates of their being Protestants & of their good behaviour but it appearing they had not paid for their several passages—

ORDERED that the Clerk do grant certificates to Messrs. Torrans Pouag and Co. who were empowered by the owners of the ship they came in to receive the same.

Read also the following Petitions praying for the Bounty allowed by the said Act VIZ

	Ages
James Gray	33
Martha Walker	15
Thomas Walker	7
John Walker	14
Samuel Walker	12

The Petitioners produced proper Certificates of their good behaviour but it appearing they had not paid for their passages ORDERED that the Certificates be delivered to Messrs Torrans Pouag & Co. as above.

Read also the following petitions praying for the Bounty allowed by the said Act

	Ages		Ages
Jane Lesslie	40	Catherine Moore	33
Ann Lesslie	13	Ann Moore	14
Wm. Lesslie	8	Hugh Moore	13
Mart Lesslie	11	James Moore	10
Thomas Lesslie	5	William Moore	2
Jane Lesslie	2	Jannet Walker	38
Mary Lesslie	38	Jane Maxwell	28
Wm. Lesslie	13	Robert Maxwell	12
Jane Lesslie	11	Alex'dr Maxwell	10
Samuel Lesslie	7	John Maxwell	8
John Lesslie	4	Nicholas Maxwell	5
Eliz'h Webb	30	Mary Webb	14
Andrew Webb	10	Sarah Webb	6
John Webb	2	Sarah McClue	26
Barbara McClue	2	Martha Crossley	30
Ann Crossley	15	Mary Crossley	9
Susannah Crossley	7	Bridget McCormack	20

	Ages		
Martha Mather	18	100	acres
Sarah Lacey	18	100	”
John Black	16	100	”
Andrew Beryhill	18	100	”

The Petitioners severally producing certificates of their being protestants & also of their good behaviour & receipts for their passages ORDERED that the Clerk do grant them Certificates to the Public Treasurer to pay them the several Bounties allowed by the said Act

Read also the petitions of the following Protestants lately arrived from Great Britain praying for Warrants of Survey & the Bounty VIZ

Acres

Donald Harper

100 In Boonesborough or Belfast Township

James Gaillard

100 ”   ”   ”   ”   ”

Lawrence Hutchins

350 In or near Orangeburg Township.

Samuel Kingwood

200 ”   ”   ”   ”   ”

ORDERED that the Secretary do prepare Warrants of Survey & that the Clerk do grant Certificates to the Public Treasurer, to pay them Bounty as prayed for by the petitions.

Read also the following Petitions praying for the Bounty VIZ

	Age
Sarah Hutchins	38 years
Alice Hutchins	7 ”
Martha Kingwood	40 ”
Rich'd Walter Hutchins	11 ”
Mary Hutchins	4 ”
Jacob Kingwood	11 ”

And they producing proper Certificates & receipts for their Passages ORDERED that the Clerk do grant them Certificates to the Public Treasurer agreeable to the directions of the said Act.

COUNCIL JOURNAL 32, page 677.
Meeting of 9 December 1765.

His Honor the Lieutenant Governor also informed the Board that some of the Irish people who lately arrived in this province on the Bounty and whose orders for the same had been made payable to Messrs. Torrans, Pouag & Co., in consideration for their passages had been with him and set forth that they apprehended they were entitled the twenty shillings sterling provided by the said Act for to buy them tools and Mr. Pouag attending was called in and produced an assignment for their

Bounty generally value received by them in their passage to this place. The Board upon recourse had to the Act were of opinion that they were not authorized under it to give orders in consideration of their passages for more than the four pounds sterling and as the assignment was a matter proper for a private litigation it was out of their province to meddle with it.

COUNCIL JOURNAL 32, page 709-710.

Meeting of 31 January 1766.

Read the following Petitions praying for Warrants of Land on the Bounty, viz

	Acres	
Abraham Pearce	100	
John Thorpe	100	
John Kinder	100	
James McPherson	100	On or near the Long Canes
John Michael	100	
Robert Hall	100	
John Seyler	100	
David Seyler	100	At the Congarees
Angelica Heyley	100	
John Purvis	100	Near the Long Canes
John Whitaker	350	ditto
John Blake	250	
Anne Blake	100	

The petitioners severally alleged that they were protestants and produced proper Certificates of their good behaviour and praying that they might have Orders to the public Treasurer

to pay them the Bounties allowed by the Act of the General
Assembly passd 25th. July 1761.

ORDERED that the Clerk do issue Certificates to them agreeable to the prayers of their Petitions.

Read also the following Petitions praying for Certificates
for the Bounty—

Mary Blake	aged 45	years
Marg't Whitaker	" 38	"
Frances Whitaker	" 11	"
Alice Blake	" 12	"
Rachel Whitaker	" 15	"
Marg't Whitaker	" 7	"
William Whitaker	" 3	"

ORDERED that the Clerk do issue Certificates to them
agreeable to the prayers of the Petitions.

COUNCIL JOURNAL 32, page 712.

Meeting of 13th. February 1766.

The following Petitions praying for Warrants of Survey for
lands and the Bounty given by the Act of the General Assembly
passed the 25th. day of July 1761, were presented and read, viz.

	Acres	
Frederick Glass	350	
Donald McGilvray	100	
William Clemmick	150	
Charles Crow	100	
John Hume	100	At or near the Long Canes.
John Lyon	100	
William Marks	100	
Philip Stock	100	

ORDERED that the Secretary do prepare Warrants of Survey and the Clerk do issue Certificates to the public Treasurer to pay them the Bounty agreeable to the prayers of their Petitions.

Read also Petitions of the following persons praying to be allowd the said Bounty, viz.

	Age
Mary Glass	25
John Glass	10
Mary Glass	9
Catherine Glass	6
Sarah Glass	4
Mary Clennick	27
Francis Cran	10

ORDERED that the Clerk do grant them the Certificates as prayed for by their respective Petitions.

COUNCIL JOURNAL 32, pages 713-727.
Meeting of 13th. February 1766.

The humble petition of Isaac Lascelles Winn
SHEWETH

That your petitioner arrived in this Province about four weeks ago with the ship Frankland under his command haveing on board of her one hundred and sixty eight poor German protestants a list of whose respective names and ages are hereunto annexed.

That your Petitioner has set on shore and disposed of to persons here the said German protestants who respectively have paid to or settled with your petitioner for the several sums due to the ship for their passages from Germany to America exclusive of the Bounty given by the Act of the General Assembly of this Province passed the 25th. July 1761 to be paid to the Masters of the ships who shall bring them into this Province they not having previously paid for their passages

Your Petitioner therefore humbly prays for your Honor Order to the Public Treasurer to pay to him the several Bounties of four pounds and two pounds sterling according to their respective ages of the said Protestants agreeable to the directions of the said Act.

And he as in duty bound will ever pray.

Isaac Lascelles Winn

Names	Ages	Names	Ages
Johannes Peter	40	Andreas Bouterwick	21
Johannes Waltman	27	Andreas Casburger	50
Andreas Kourman	30	Elizabeth Embrigen	32
George Myer	18	Katherine Kruderith	25
Andrew Claiter	17	Dan Sagual	36
Hans Yorrick Coastre	23	Hannah Roylick	22
George Kerner	23	Ursula Bursula	30
Hans Yorrick Myer	18	Christian Sazer	39
Nicholas Keyester	25	Mich'l Wolf	39
John Adam Kygall	16	Eva Wolf	19
Conrad Myer	15	Valentine Frank	39
Bernard Sleiger	15	Michael Frank	15
Peter Craymer	40	Anna Maria Werrell	22
Francis Dourfour	27	Christopher Horner	43
Michael Kerbs	18	Andrew Brigure	40
Aaron Kaufman	28	Anna Brigure	19
Ber Admitz	18	Johan Merwitz	38
Andrew Bonet	21	Kahlba Merwitz	22
Jared Finerman	30	Murza Merwitz	5
Andrew Englet	24	Jeremiah Copnal	26
Constantine Falman	27	John George Keleigh	32
Christopher Snalman	21	Maria Dorothea Keleigh	28
Joseph Lirister	30	Eva Keleigh	9
Peter Halgerman	25	Nannella DeSaugre	24
Hanrick Mellett	23	Math. Camster	34
Johan Killerman	32	Marg't Hoodsman	21
Jacob Menningon	30	Adam Carresford	28
Johan George Kleist	32	Anna Maria Kerlesford	26
Catherine Calbrindon	21	Fred'k Carrlesford	9
Michael Reymor	22	Johannes Seyferts	30
John Balker Hartmutz	19	Anna Christian Seyferts	28
Johan Keynal	18	Silvanus Seyferts	10
Jacob Richman	28	Michael Winter	41
Anna Maria Kruld	23	Anna Marg'tha Winter	27
Dorothea Knarl	18	Nicholas Heyder	29
Peter Mike	36	John Underbrank	32
Yorrick Lodowick Wyler	36	Anna Maria Underbrank	21

	Ages		Ages
Andreas Gosselin	28	Margaretta Fink	50
Barbara Gosselin	20	Michael Carrell	43
Valentine Groo	25	Margaretta Carrell	42
Teresia Groo	25	Christian Dorn	35
Johannes Alvander	22	Margaretta Dorn	30
Johannes Cree	24	Johannes Skelck	38
Martilla Grey	17	Apollonea Skeck	31
Anna Helena Heyder	29	Christian Seyler	32
Johannes Hoofidot	50	Anne Seyler	27
Anna Maria Anweider	18	Michael Merts	33
Maria Dorobat Hoofidot	39	Cunninghand Merts	31
Johan Jacob Heyler	39	Adam Brener	40
Catherine Ester Heydel	38	Catherine Brener	22
Johan Jacob Heydel	15	Johannes Hartwild	39
Anna Teresia Heydel	14	Philip Jacob Smith	31
Hester Heydell	11	Lorisia Catherine Smith	32
Werra Heydell	6	Frances Ort	29
Conrad Fred'k Heydel	4	Catherine Ort	21
John Erret	19	Henrick Mantzor	27
Stephen Kelsey	19	Elizabeth Mantzor	20
Jacob Kind	17	Joseph Walla	35
Johan Jacob Mouterer	30	Maria Walla	30
Maria Mouterer	24	Jacob Dertor	25
John W. Shoulderin	27	Anna Maria Derter	22
Maria Shoulderin	25	Peter Courants	39
Hans Yorick Chipperwick	29	Chestina Mouterer	4
Helena Chipperwick	22	Johan Chipperwick	4
Johannes Shorten	27	Johan Jacob Shorten	4
Eliz'h Shorten	27	Hans Yorick Kickart	5
Christian Fry	30	James Carril	15
Margaretta Fry	20	Lessell Carril	13
Stephanus Scholfert	28	Rosina Carril	10
Josepha Scholfert	18	Babella Carril	7
Johan Yorick Kickart	32	Dorothea Carril	5
Elsa Maria Kickart	25	Barbara Courant	35
Yorick Barnard Stey	35	Hester Dorn	8
Maria Eliz'th Stey	32	Margaretta Dorn	5
Hans Yorick Fink	30	Barbara Scherick	13
Catherine Fink	27	Christian Scherick	10

	Ages		Ages
Lena Scherick	7	Lenah Smith	7
Stephannes Motte	8	Rachel Smith	5
Yorick Mert	7	Leta Ort	5
Maria Eva Mert	5	John Yorick Wella	8
John Jacob Hartwild	7	Cornelius Wella	6
Petrus Hartwild	5	Lucet Courents	15
Hanna Margaretta Smith	8	Frederick Courents	13

ORDERED that the public Treasurer do pay to the said Isaac Lascelles Winn the Bounty of Four pounds and two pounds sterling according to the respective ages of the said protestants and to themselves the Bounty of twenty shillings sterling, agreeable to the directions of the said Act.

Read also the following petition of Isaac Lascelles Winn—

SOUTH CAROLINA—To the Honorable William Bull, Esq., Lieut. Governor, Commander in Chief in and over the said Province—

The humble petition of Isaac Lascelles Winn sheweth—

That your petitioner arrived in this province from Rotterdam about four weeks ago, with the ship Frankland under his command, having on board of her twenty-four Germans, a list of whose respective names are herewith annexed and whom your petitioner verily believes to be protestants.

That your petitioner permitted the said Germans to go on shore in this Province on several people to whom they respectively articled themselves paying to him a sum of money as a part consideration for their passages, and an assignment of the Bounty allowed by this Province for the remainder. That they were all severally disposed of before your petitioner was informed that it was customary for the said Germans to be sworn to their allegiance.

He therefore humbly prays that he may have an order to the public Treasurer to pay him the said Bounty.

And he is in duty bound will ever pray.

Isaac Lascelles Winn.

	Ages		Ages
Johannes Worresdect	13	Anthon Snell	22
Theodosia Wolt	12	John Seyfers	22
Catherine Retz	8	Conrad Werts	40
Unamia Hortwoldt	8	Eva Werts	30
Christopher (has forgot		Hans Jacob, their son	14
his sirname)	14	Herod Weylens	36
Peter Crouse	19	Guesta Weylens	35
Joseph Brener	20	Mertilla, their daughter,	14
Christopher Pens	26	Johannes Schlester	28
Leonard Stamler	28	Andreas Tanfert	22
Barnard Carl	15	Hans Gorrie Grafhert	19
Eliz'h Kinnlingsen	14	Lena Pens	18
James Woresdie	15		

Read also the petitions of the following persons setting forth that they were lately arrived in this Province on the encouragement of the Bounty and therefore humbly praying for Warrants of survey and the Bounty, viz:

	Acres	
Jacob Lockyer	150	In or near Londonborough Township.
Christian Hasseroot	100	" " " " "
John Nicholas Werreck	150	" " " " "
Michael Motte	100	" " " " "

ORDERED that the Secretary do prepare Warrants of survey and that the Clerk do issue certificates to the public Treasurer to pay them the Bounties prayed for by the petitions.

Read also petitions of Barbara Lockyer and Maria Eva Werrick, praying for certificates to the public Treasurer to pay them the Bounty.

ORDERED that the Clerk do issue the certificates as prayed for.

Council Journal 32, pages 734-736
Meeting of March 31, 1766

Read the following Petitions of the poor protestants lately arrived from Ireland on the encouragement of the Bounty given by this Province and praying for the same and Warrants of survey of lands.

	Ages	Acres
Arthur Dixon	21	100
John Lowry	18	100
David Blake	34	350
Josias Carrs	30	100
William Blair	27	100
Robert McCamick	31	100
John Bodle	18	100
Robert Stewart	22	100
John Forster	18	100
Anthony Clinton	17	100
Andrew Anclerson	15	100
Samuel Bodle	15	100
John McDowal	24	100
Richard Manning	21	100
Thomas Connolly	21	100
Patrick McMullen	28	100
John McElroy	17	100
Bartholomew McA Fee	20	100
Patrick Dick	42	100
James Crawford	40	300
Joseph Crawford	21	100
Marg't Crawford	16	100
John McElvie	15	100
James Martin	62	100
Robert Martin	26	100
George Blair	16	100
Mary McCardell	27	100
William Reily	48	100
Joseph McMullens	21	100
Patrick Dick	43	100
David Gray	22	100
Samuel McGill	23	100
Sarah Hans Johnston	18	100
William Nugent	21	100
James Kennedy	21	100
Susanna Kaine	38	100
John Kain	14	100

	Ages	Acres
Hannah Hory	18	100
William McFerral	22	100
Mary Eddy	12	100
John Rowan	21	100
Letitia Wilson	18	100
Catherine Faulkner	12	100
Robert Pootts	20	100
Joseph Jolly	20	100
Mary Burns	30	100
Robert Beetsome	28	100
Ann Faulkner	28	100
Elizabeth Dart	20	100
Catherine Blundell	18	100
James McMelen	22	100

In Boonesborough or Belfast Townships. The Petitioners severally produced their Certificates of their being protestants & prayed to be allowed the Bounty given by the Act of the General Assembly of this Province passed 25th July 1761

ORDERED that the Clerk do grant them certificates agreeable to the prayers of their petitions.

COUNCIL JOURNAL 32, page 777.
Meeting of 6th. June 1766.

Read the following petitions praying for Warrants of Survey on the Bounty—

Jane Gilbert	100	
Elias Gendernes	100	
Ann Gilbair	100	
Francis Duplici	100	
Lewis Borell	150	In Hillsborough Township.
Mary Borell	100	
Jane Miot	100	
Ann Macguire	100	

The Petitioners also set forth that they were Protestants and lately come into this province on the Encouragement of the Bounty given by the Act of the General Assembly of this Province passed the 25th July 1761 and therefore humbly praying the same but it appearing they had not paid nor satisfied the owners of the ship for their passages—

ORDERED that the Clerk do deliver their Certificates to James Straien Commander of the ship London agreeable to the directions of the said Act and that the Secretary do prepare Warrants of Survey as prayed for by the Petitioners.

Read the following petitions on the Bounty—
Jacob Bouler 100 acres in Hillsborough Township
Hanna Eva 100 acres   ”   ”   ”

ORDERED that the Clerk do issue Certificates to the public Treasurer and to the Secretary to prepare Warrants of Survey accordingly.

COUNCIL JOURNAL 32, page 804-809.
Meeting of 11th. July 1766.

Read the following Petitions for Warrants of Survey......
.... On the Bounty—

Christopher Tachtman   250 acres at the Long Canes and the Bounty given by the Act of the General Assembly passed the 25th. July 1761.

ORDERED that the Public Treasurer do pay him the Bounty and that the Secretary do prepare Warrants of Survey as prayed for by the Petitions.

Read also the following Petitions praying for the Bounty

	Ages
Margaret Tachtman	32
Margaret Tachtman	3
Elizabeth King	20

The petitioners producing Certificates of their being protestants and discharges for their passages

ORDERED that the Clerk do issue Certificates to the public Treasurer to pay them the Bounty allowed by the said Act.

60

Council Journal 32, page 830-831.
Meeting of 2nd. October 1766.

The following Petitions for Warrants of Survey on the Bounty were presented and read, Viz't—

Robert Patterson	150 on the branches of Santee and the Bounty allowed by the Act of the General Assembly Passed the 25th. day of July 1761.
Peter Dorst	100 on Santee or Savannah River.

Esther Patterson for the Bounty allowed to protestants settling in this province by the Act of the General Assembly passed 25th. July 1761

ORDERED that the Secretary do prepare Warrants of Survey and that the Clerk do grant Certificates to the Public Treasurer to pay the said Robert Patterson and Esther Patterson the Bounty allowed by the said Act.

Council Journal 32, page 842-846.
Meeting of 17th. October 1766.

The Petitions on the Bounty were presented and read viz.

Names	Acres	Names	Acres
Anna Barbara Gilbert	250	Eva Cahfmannin	250
Hans George Flick	200	Jacob Schyner	150
John Diouck Boehn	150	Jacob Geysler	250
Barbara Riggen	100	George Philip Zehuder	150
Jacob Lang	100	Hans Adam Kerber	100
Maria Christian Lang	150	Casper Springer	100
Regina Steyhen	100	Michael Thirry	300
Irig Adam Kibler	100	John Jacob Beidinger	200
George Philip Getn	100	Michael Hunsinger	100
Nicholas Ruth	100	Gotleb Ebinger	100
Henrick Eyksteyt	150	Jacob Writzell	250
Sebastian Schemdst	300	Wolfcomb Writzell	100
Solomon Schyner	350	Mary Mad'n Eyhsteen	150
Jacob Voltrall	150	Christopher Metz	300
Daniel Keller	250	Francis Hero	250
Adam Gutt	200	Anna Maria Heyhen	100
Hans George Patt	150	Johannes Peltzer	100

Names	Acres	Names	Acres
John Willin Bader	100	Christian Willherring	100
Robert Dinah	100	Jacob Kolshire	150
Jacob Worm	150	Anna Christian Setzler	100
John Schneatter	200	Johannes Setzler	400
Peter Keller	250	George Adam Yan	150
Benedictus Nonnemaker	150	John Peter Peysell	100
George Zachary Herring	100	Hans Peysell	100
John George Herring	100	Johan Mich'l Scherman	100
Anna Elizabeth Herring	100	Francis Schover	150
Anthony Rets	200	Peter Setzler	200
Johan Joost Schaffer	150	Eva Catherine Pracht	250
Jacob Morrow	150	Johan Nichol Pracht	100
Laurence Estyhens	150	George Adam Schumpert	100
Johannes Hoppell	150	John Jacob Schumpert	100
Hans George Kress	150	Jacob Schumpert	250
Jacob Kulmany	150	Catherine Hoofmanin	100
Eprosina Hansilmanin	100	Casper Bless	150
Lucius Schihen	100	Joseph Chel	150
Philip Awl	100	Philip Jacob Behler	350
Johannes Hauck	100	Diedrick Uts	250
George Rothmeyer	300	Anna Margaret Utsin	100
Erhert Rothmeyer	100	John Jacob Webler	100
Eva Maria Rothmeyer	100	Michael Webler	300
Ursula Bartholomanin	100	John George Winburger	350
Maria Catherine Hering	100	Johan Philip Zimmerle	100
John Wellen Ropsher	300	Mary Eliz'h Zimmerle	100
John Adam Irrig	150	Anna Marg't Zimmerle	100
John Michael Bredenger	150	John Jacob Zimmerle	100
Conrad Immick	300	Hans Zimmerle	400
Jacob Herr	150	Thomas Lang	350
Frederick Irrig	150	Elizabeth Klingmanin	150
Jacob Irrig	100	Johannes Schem	150
Conrad Minger	100	Johannes Nicholas Young	100
Peter Keysher	100	Henrick Young	300
Carl Frederick Frolick	200	Johan Jacob Knough	100
Anna Maria Kusterin	100	Henrick Knough	350
Catherine Merking	100	Andreas Scruber	250
Philip Seigle	100	Dorothea Samblin	100
Petrus Balbris	100	Hans Mich'l Kubler	300

Names	Acres	Names	Acres
Johannes Schaufferberger	150	Anna Marg't Fan	100
Andreas Schimst	150	Catherine Ratherin	150
Johan Christian Schroder	150	Andreas Keller	850
Christopher Krahner	150	Johannes Adam Mickell	100
Johannes Hern	200	John George Rarick	100
Henrick Guess	800	Anna Belonia Knight	100
Johannes Skilling	100	Ann Maria Fisherin	100
Jacob Zimmerman	200	Elizabeth Emekin	100

Between Broad and Savannah Rivers.

ORDERED that the Secretary do prepare Warrants of Survey as prayed for by the petitioners.

The Petitioners also set forth that they were protestants arrived in this province in the ship Britannia from Amsterdam on the encouragement and Bounty given by the Act of the General Assembly passed the 25th. July 1761.

COUNCIL JOURNAL 32, pages 846-850
Meeting of October 17, 1766.

The following persons also presented to his Excellency petitions setting forth that they were severally protestants and had come into this Province from Germany on the Bounty and encouragement given to foreign protestants who shall come from Europe to reside in this Province by the Act of the General Assembly of this Province passed the 25th. July 1761.

	Ages		Ages
Grassanha Zimmerle	35	Johannes Jacob Kubler	5
Anna Zimmerle	6	Catherine Kubler	3
Anna Margaretta Geys	12	Anna Maria Schober	36
Catherine Geys	9	Anna Maria Schober	15
Elizabeth Geys	4	Maria Eliz'h Scober	12
Ursula Krahner	21	Anna Magdelin Knight	36
Philip Jacob Geys	12	Anna Belonia Knight	15
Elizabeth Schroder	29	Anna Catherine Knight	11
Catherine Schimsdt	25	Maria Eliz'h Knight	9
Ann Spasia Schaufferberger	26	Maria Catherine Knight	2
Anna Marg'a Kubler	45	Margaretta Joor	39
Elizabeth Kubler	9	Maria Elizabeth Joor	14

	Ages		Ages
Margaretta Joor	10	Margaret Schover	20
Christian Joor	2	Elizabeth Jan	22
Catherine Schim	48	Ann Christian Setzler	36
Andreas Klingmanin	2½	John George Setzler	12
Maria Eliz'h Lang	26	George Adam Setzler	15
Maria Christian Lang	9	Ann Elizabeth Setzler	3
Johannes Martin Lang	7	John Adam Setzler	10
Johannes Lang	4	Anna Catherine Holtshire	23
Anna Marg'ta Zimmeral	49	Maria Catherine Repscher	27
Maria Eliz'h Zimmeral	15	Maria Catherine Repscher	8
Johannes Zimmeral	11	Johan Repscher	6
Johannes Adam Zimmeral	9	Anna Margar'ta Repscher	4
Maria Catherine Zimmeral	9	Elizabeth Irrigg	25
Anna Maria Zimmeral	7	George Adam Pracht	2
Anna Catherine Wynberger	29	Christian Breydinger	18
John George Wynberger	12	Eva Emmick	37
Anna Rosina Wynberger	9	Eliz'h Emmick	14
Anna Catherine Wynberger	6	Conrad Emmick	12
Eva Catherine Wynberger	2	Anna Margaret Emmick	4
Margaret Webber	37	Eva Catherine Herr	17
Conrod Webber	8	Anna Maria Irrigg	19
Jacob Peter Webber	7	Conrad Minges	26
Charles Webber	3	Peter Keysher	19
Eva Catherine Uts	27	Eliz'h Eleonoro Frolick	30
George Peter Uts	8	Augusta Maria Frolick	5
Maria Catherine Uts	4	Elizabeth Hauck	27
Barbara Behler	30	Magdalina Hauck	9
Eva Marg'ta Behler	13	Catherine Hauck	4
Christopher Behler	11	Erhert Ruthmeyer	23
Johannes Adam Behler	7	Martin Ruthmeyer	12
Johannes Jacob Behler	4	Nicholas Ruthmeyer	9
Margaret Ches	19	Ursula Bartholomein	20
Ann Christian Schrumpert	38	Sophia Rits	18
John Peter Schrumpert	13	Christian Rits	3
Maria Eliz'h Schrumpert	8	Susannah Marg'ta Schoffer	20
Eva Catherine Pracht	26	Eliz'h Maurer	25
Eva Elizabeth Pracht	6	Anna Maria Erstern	19
Anna Maria Setzler	29	Maria Barbara Oppell	21
Anna Marg't Setzler	3	Maria Charlotte Kress	21

	Ages		Ages
Susanna Koelman	25	Christian Schynher	3
Anna Margaretta Melz	25	Ann Marg't Volhill	27
John Valentine Melz	6	Anna Marg't Keller	28
Maria Catherine Melz	4	John Keller	8
Anna Aria Eliz'h Schnetter	32	John Philip Keller	2
Philip Charles Schnetter	5	Elizabeth Gatt	19
Margaretta Keller	22	Maria Catherine Pubb	24
John George Keller	7	Eva Keller	28
Sophia Marg't Nonnemaker	18	Maria Keller	10
Anna Maria Lender	18	Theobold Keller	8
Anna Maria Thirry	32	Margaret Keller	8
John Peter Thirry	12	Mary Eliz'h Hansilmanin	12
John Michal Thirry	8	Eve Eliz'h Hauffmanin	8
John Philip Thirry	4	Leonard Hauffmanin	5
Ann Maria Brydenger	19	Catherine Schneyer	31
Linhert Brydenger	2	Maria Catherine Geysler	35
Anna Maria Wuttsull	36	Frederick Geysler	12
Eva Wuttsull	8	Eva Marg'ta Geysler	3
Martin Wuttsull	3	Hans Jacob Gilbert	34
Dorothea Esksteyn	52	John George Gilber	12
Catherine Eliz'h Estyhen	2	Anna Christian Frick	26
Anna Catherine Schimst	35	John George Frick	4
George Adam Schimst	11	Elizabeth Boem	27
Maria Christiana Schimst	8	Barbara Boem	51
Barbara Schynder	43	Maria Christian Lang	22
Barbara Schynder	11	George Henry Lang	2
Johannes Schynher	9		

ORDERED that the public Treasurer do pay the several Bountys prayed for to Mr. William Ancrum in behalf of the owners of the ship Belfast Packet which they came over in in consideration of their passages it appearing that they had not severally payd for the same.

COUNCIL JOURNAL 32, page 850-853.

Meeting of 26th. October 1766.

His Honour the Lieutenant Governor informed his Excellenty that during the interuption giveing to Public Business by the Stamp Acts being prevented from operating several vessels had arrived from Europe with settlers on the encouragement and Bounty given by this Province and as Warrants of Survey could not then be issued for their Lands they had been sent into the Country to settle on such Lands that are vacant as they could find that as soon as the Stamp Act was repealed (to wit) on the sixth of May last their Warrants were issued but they had not takeing them out of the Surveyor General Office as the hot weather had probably prevented their comeing to Town and that the time for Executing them was now near expireing Whereupon the Board advised His Excellency to give orders to the Surveyor General to prolong such of the said Warrants as were now lying in the Office for six months from the date hereof which his Excellency was pleased to do accordingly.

Council Journal 32, page 851.

Meeting of 26 October 1766.

The following Petitions for Warrants of Survey on the Bounty were presented and read.

	Acres		Acres
William Woodall	400	James Montgomery	100
James Wells	150	Thomas Clark	100
William Still	100	Michael Fegart	100
William Gibson	100	John Owens	200
James Johnston	100	Dominick Johnston	100
Elizabeth Ash	100	William Wilson	200
Patrick McCann	100	Nathaniel Wilson	100
Randall McCallaster	100	Jane Wilson	100
Edward McHibler	100	Sarah Wilson	100
Robert Bennett	100	Mary Wilson	100
David Cockran	100	Mary Summerville	100
James Simson	300	Hugh Summerville	100
John Simson	100	George Summerville	100
Michal Darby	100	Isabel Summerville	100
James McCann	100	Margaret Wilson	100
Patrick McCann	100	Robert Heartly	100
James Graham	100	John Davies	100
James McQuoid	100	Andrew Ross	200
Terry Quinn	100	Agnes Still	100

	Acres		Acres
Mary Parkinson	100	John Hearse, Jun'r	100
James Hewitt	100	Terrance McQuire	150
James Frazier	100	Peter McQuire	100
William Shannon	100	Samuel Swan	200
John Hearse	400		

At or near the Long Canes.

And they producing proper Certificates and also receipts for their respective passages It is ORDERED that the Secretary do prepare Warrants of Survey and that the Clerk do issue his Certificate to the Public Treasurer to pay them the Bounty allowed by the said Act.

COUNCIL JOURNAL 33, page 40.
Meeting of 19 February 1767.

The undermentioned persons presented petitions to his Excellency the Governor setting forth that they respectively were Protestants and had lately come over into this Province from Great Britain on the encouragement and Bounty given by the Act of the General Assembly of this Province passed the 25th of July 1761 and therefore prayed for Warrants of Survey and grants for land free of charge and the Bounty given by the said Act and producing proper Certificates and discharges for their passages, it is ordered that the Secretary do prepare Warrants of Survey to the Petitioners.

Thomas Jones	100	
Thomas Gelley	100	
William Sheralton	100	In Granville County.
John Bull	100	
John James	100	

And that the Public Treasurer do pay them the Bounty allowed by the said Act.

COUNCIL JOURNAL 33, page 41-50.
Meeting of 27th. February 1767.

His Excellency informed the Board that a vessel with poor
Irish protestants had lately arrived here on the encouragement
of the Bounty given by the Act of the General Assembly passed
the 25th July 1761 and that he had now directed them to attend and they being called into the Council Chamber they presented the following Petitions for Warrants of Survey for Land
on the Bounty VIZ'T

	Acres		Acres
John Montgomery	300	John Cameron	250
Andrew Youart	300	Samuel Leard	300
John Kennedy	150	Mathew Shanks	150
Alexander McBride	300	David Pressley	350
James Youart	250	William Hanvey	250
Arthur Watts	100	John McFarlan	350
Thomas Watts	400	George McComb	150
John Lindsey	250	Christopher Russell	250
Andrew Youart	150	William Thomson	150
Robert Boggs	200	Robert McCrachen	150
William Little	100	James Wood	150
Thomas Ross	100	Robert Reid	500
Jane Ross	100	James Mordack	200
William Ross	150	William Sloan	200
John Mordack	350	Alexander Forster	150
John Jones	250	John Anderson	300
William Anderson	200	Thomas Humphreys	200
Henry Linden	150	Mary Humphreys	100
John Wright	200	Jane Humphreys	100
Isabella Lindsey	100	John Humphreys	100
Samuel Lindsey	100	John Patterson	100
John Wright	200	Josias Patterson	100
James Ellis	150	James Patterson	250
Catherine McAdam	250	James Major	300
David Willey	150	John Major	100
Moses Bradford	100	William Major	100
Thomas Bradford	150	Thomas Lindsey	400
John Bradford	150	John Bennison	200
Neal Raverty	250	William Bennison	100

	Acres		Acres
Fanny Bennison	100	George Johnston	100
Agnes Crosier	150	Samuel Boggs	100
James Crosier	100	William Gibson	100
Mary Crosier	100	Henry Montgomery	100
Thomas Crosier	100	James Greer	100
Sarah Crosier	100	Thomas Dickson	100
James Miscampble	250	James Moore	100
John Miscampble	100	John Sims	100
Elizabeth Kirkwood	250	Thomas Turner	100
Robert Young	100	James Graham	100
Elizabeth Young	100	Samuel Arnot	100
Samuel Young	100	John Ingram	100
Margaret Gray	200	Mary Harvey	100
Jane Gray	100	Samuel Bruce	100
Archibald Porter	100	William Purse	100
Alexander Porter	100	John Hughes	100
William Baillie	100	James McWilliams	100
James Patterson	100	John McElwean	100
Edward Herthrington	100	Samuel Foster	100
George McCulloch	100	William Robinson	100
Thomas Nellson	100	John Gibson	100
Samuel Dickson	100	Hugh Porter	100
Patrick Bell	100	Agnes Bradford	100
James Heron	100	Samuel Lindsay	100
Robert Beath	100	John Young	100
Alexander Robinson	100	Andrew Crosier	100
Mary Brown	100	Andrew Reed	100
William McGuire	100	Hugh McCormack	100

In Boonesborough or Belfast Township.

ORDERED that the Secretary do prepare Warrants of Survey on the Bounty agreeable to the prayers of their petitions and that the public Treasurer do pay the Bounties given by the said Act to Messrs. Torrans and Pouag and Mr. Robert Bath for the owners of the ship Hillsborough in consideration of their passages to the said province agreeable to the directions of the said Act.

The following persons also presented petitions setting forth that they were protestants and had come into this Province in

the said ship Earl of Hillsborough on the encouragement of the
said Act and therefore prayed to be allowed the Bounty given
by the same.

	Ages		Ages
Marg't Kennedy	35	Margaret Watts	12
Mary Yourat	30	Andrew Watts	6
James McCradam	13	Thomas Watts	4
John Cameron	8	Margaret Murdagh	35
Marg't Cameron	5	Joseph Murdagh	7
Mary Miscampble	30	Mary Murdagh	6
James Miscampble	15	Elizabeth Murdagh	3
Robert Miscampble	9	Marther Ross	25
Robert Kirkwood	15	Margaret Willey	25
James Kirkwood	13	Catherine McCadam	26
Mary McBride	33	John McCadam	10
James McBride	8	Catherine McCadam	7
Andrew McBridge	3	James McCadam	2
Elizabeth Boggs	33	Isabell Ellis	26
Elizabeth Boggs	10	Arabella Linder	21
Jannett Young	45	Alexander Anderson	8
Robert Bath	17	Mary Anderson	6
Samuel Young	7	John Anderson	1
Martha Forster	21	Agnes Jones	35
Elizabeth Youart	25	James Johns	13
Samuel Youart	2	John Jones	7
Mary Youart	6	Jannet Reid	4
Rachel Montgomery	30	William Reid	12
Samuel Montgomery	13	Mary Reid	8
William Montgomery	12	Sarah Reid	5
Latitia Montgomery	9	Hannah Reid	3
Rachel Youart	60	Agnes Murdagh	25
Sarah Bennison	45	Jannett Murdack	4
George Bennison	14	Margaret Wright	26
Agnes Lindsey	35	Agnes Slone	29
John Lindsey	7	Thomas Slone	3
Robert Lindsey	5	Ann Branford	58
Elizabeth Lindley	3	Mary Raverty	45
Sarah Watts	35	Margaret Raverty	10
James Watts	14	Malcolm Raverty	8

	Ages		Ages
Jellie Camron	46	Rebecca McCombe	21
James Camron	13	Eliz'h Major	35
Margaret Camron	17	David Major	13
Agnes Humphries	40	Mary Major	15
Agnes Humphries	11	Jane Russell	34
Jane Patterson	40	Ester Major	7
Alexander Patterson	14	Mary Russel	8
Agnes Patterson	13	Martha Russel	3
Margaret Laird	36	Eliz'h Lindsay	35
John Laird	6	Agnes Lindsay	13
Mary Laird	4	Eliz'h Lindsay	4
Samuel Laird	2	Thomas Lindsay	1
James Shanks	3	James Lindsay	3
Ester Plessley	36	Elizabeth Thomson	25
Samuel Plessley	11	Jane McCrahen	30
David Pressley	6	Jane Wood	30
Agnes Pressley	4	Isabell Wood	25
Sarah Hanvey	26	William Anderson	6
Jane Hanvey	3	Elizabeth Anderson	2
Rose McParlin	36	Elizabeth Porter	25
Archibald McParlin	7	Margaret Gray	14
Jane McParlin	5	James Patterson	25
George McParlin	3		

The Petitioners set forth that they were protestants and that they had lately arrived in this Province on the encouragement of the Bounty given by the Act of the General Assembly of this Province passed the 25th. July 1761 and therefore praying the same and they haveing severally produced Certificates required by the Act

IT WAS ORDERED that the public Treasurer do pay the several Bounties to Messrs. Torrans and Pouag and Bath in Consideration for their passages in the said Ship.

COUNCIL JOURNAL 33, page 145.
Meeting of 28 May, 1767.

The following petitions for Warrants of Survey on the Bounty were read, viz.

	Acres		Acres
Thomas Campbell	200	James Wilson	100
Mary Campbell	100	Thomas Johnston	100
George Campbell	100	James Ballentine	100
Margaret Campbell	100	James Greer	100
Jacob Hart	300	William Leithgon	200
William Archier	350	James Cooks	350
Robert Archier	100	William Atkinson	350
Francis Gillion	250	Simon Kelly	400
Abram Jones	400	Joseph Kelly	100
Ann Jones	100	Thomas Stell	200
David Jones	100	Violet Allen	100
Andrew Reynolds	250	William Shankley	150
David Brown	150	Robert Henning	350
John Magilton	100	James Henning	100
Andrew Herman	150	Michael Henning	100
James Morfatt	400	Abraham Wright	100
John Carmichael	100	Mary Proctor	150
Francis Campbell	100	Patrick Conn	100
Margaret Campbell	100	Alexander Vernon	100
Jannet Campbell	100	Richard Davis	100
Mary Campbell	100	James McCrahen	100
Alexander Campbell	100	Alexander McDowell	200
Elizabeth Campbell	100	Andrew McDowell	100
Samuel Hamilton	250	James McDowell	100
John Knox	100	William Keys	100
Jane Henning	100	Lesslie Bill	100
Alexander Burnside	300	Margaret Bill	200
Jannet Arnet	150	James Knox	450
Robert Fleming	100	John Knox	100
Ralph Fleming	100	James Knox	100
John Sanderson	150	Jannet Knox	100
Henry McCallon	150	Robert Jones	200
William Magilton	100	Joseph Jones	100
John Gibson	100	Andrew Jones	100
James Gibson	100	William Jones	100
William Gibson	100	Andrew Adair	450
Edward Miskilly	100	Alice Adair	100
John Cameron	100	John Magee	100
Colin Forbes	200	David Tennant	300

	Acres		Acres
Thomas Watson	100	Hugh Harkins	150
James Waugh	100	John Roe	250
James Lewis	100	Samuel McMurray	100
William Smilie	100	George Arnot	100
William Brown	100	Hugh Thomson	150
Samuel Nesbitt	350	William Martin	100
Thomas Fardor	150	Malcom Kays	150
James Croll	100	Dennis Skallon	100
Samuel Clowny	100	Hugh Gregg	100
John Calhoun	100	William McDowell	100
Samuel Shannon	100	Thomas Maginsay	100
George Fleming	100	Daniel O'Neal	100
Sarah Lindsey	100	Joshua Carrol	100
Margaret Buckanan	100	Robert Egar	100
James Beaty	100	Jane Arnot	100
Nicholas Dickson	400	Moses Jameison	100
Robert Jones	100	Nicholas Lee	100
William Corrie	350	Andrew Stevenson	100
Alexander Corrie	100	John Lowrey	100
Nicholas Corrie	100	Jane Lindsay	100
John Milligan	100	Thomas Patterson	100
Isaac Crayton	100	William Burnside	100

In Boonesborough or Belfast Township.

ORDERED that the Secretary do prepare Warrants of Survey on the Bounty as prayed for by the Petitioners.

The petitioners also humbly prayed to be allowed the Bounty given by the Act of the General Assembly of this Province passed the 25th. July 1761 and they severally producing proper Certificates it was Ordered that the Public Treasurer do pay to them the Bounty allowed by the said Act.

COUNCIL JOURNAL No. 33, page 150-157.
Meeting of 28 May 1767.

The following persons also presented petitions setting forth that they were protestants and had arrived in this province on the Encouragement and bounty given by this Province and they severally producing Certificates of the same it was Ordered that

the Public Treasurer do pay them the several Bounties thereby
given as prayed for by their respective petitions.

Elizabeth Campbell
Susannah Hart
George Hart
Elizabeth Hart
Susannah Hart
Isobella Archier
Rose Archier
Ann Archier
Mary Archier
Isobella Archier
Jane Gillion
Martha Gillion
Jane Jones
Ann Jones
William Jones
Elizabeth Jones
Mary Jones
Jane Jones
Samuel Jones
Margaret Reynolds
William Reynolds
Henry Reynolds
James Reynolds
Christian Herman
Margaret Morffat
Elizabeth Morffat
Griffen Morffat
Jannett Morfat
Thomas Morffat
William Morffatt
Lilly Hamilton
Samuel Hamilton
Agnes Hamilton
Mary Burnside
William Burnside
Joseph Burnside
Mary Burnside
Margaret Burnside

Mary Sanderson
Margaret McCallon
Jane Ford
Mary Ford
Elizabeth Lethgow
Rother Lethgon
Ann Cook
Eleanor Cook
John Cock
Jane Atkinson
John Atkinson
Henry Atkinson
Elizabeth Killy
John Killy
Robert Killy
Elizabeth Killy
Mary Killy
Samuel Killy
Jane Steel
Thomas Shanley
Anne Henning
Jane Henning
Mary Henning
Ann Henning
Robert Henning
Hannah Henning
Charity Proctor
Jane McDowell
Elizabeth McDowell
William Bill
Elizabeth Knox
William Knox
Samuel Knox
Elizabeth Knox
Joseph Knox
Robert Knox
Margaret Knox
Robert Jones

Elizabeth Jones
John Johns
Mary Adair
Alex'dr Adair
James Adair
Margaret Adair
Rebecca Tennant
Margaret Nesbitt
Thomas Nesbitt
Elizabeth Nesbitt
John Nesbitt
Baddy Fardor
Margaret Dickson
James Dickson
Sarah Dickson

William Dickson
Jane Dickson
Robert Dickson
Margaret Corrie
Margaret Corrie
Robert Corrie
Jane Corrie
William Corrie
Elizabeth Harkins
Elizabeth Roe
Martha Arnot
Susannah Roe
Jane McMurray
Agnes Arnot

COUNCIL JOURNAL 33, page 178-184
Meeting of June 22, 1767.

The following petitions for Warrants of survey on the Bounty were presented and read, viz

	Acres		Acres
James Robinson	350	Sarah Morrison	100
Mary Jameison	100	Margaret Morrison	100
Grizil Jameison	100	Robert Morrison	100
Ann Jordan	100	Philip Bracking	250
James Rainey	100	Hugh McCann	250
James Cunningham	250	James McKelvey	350
Jane Cunningham	100	James McKelvey	100
James Cunningham	250	Robert Poocock	250
James Russell	200	Hugh Kimble	250
Martha Russell	100	John Ard	250
William Hay	250	John Conn	100
Samuel Knox	100	William Turk	200
James McCan	100	John Turk	100
Robert Boyd	300	Mathew Reid	200
William Boyd	100	Jannet Turk	100
James McCulloch	100	James Reid	300
James Smith	100	John Gamble	100
John Smith	100	Samuel Gamble	100

	Acres		Acres
James Gamble	100	Robert Moore	100
Martha Jordan	200	Martha Moore	100
Jane Jordan	100	Alexander Hamilton	100
Isabell Jordan	100	Joseph Neilson	100
Thomas Jordan	100	Robert Wiseman	250
Jannet Rodgers	200	Hugh Wiseman	100
William Andrews	300	Mary Ann Wiseman	100
Samuel Mark	250	James Lawfin	150
Samuel Woodside	200	Samuel Lawfin	100
Nathaniel Boyd	200	Mary Loan	100
John McBirney	250	James Loan	100
Abraham Mule	100	William Sale	100
James Hambleton	100	David Kennedy	100
Francis Rodeman	100	David Black	250
William Boyd	100	James Johnston	250
Jane Boyd	100	Robert Johnston	100
John Cox	150	John Copland	100
John Duncan	100	James McDougal	100
John Foster	200	James Develin	100
Ann Wilson	100	Robert Dennise	100
Walter Stewart	100	James McMullen	100
Hannah Jameison	100	Mathew Bell	150
Samuel Forster	100	James Campbell	100
George Craig	150	William Bonnar	150
Elizabeth Craig	100	David Lockhart	150
Mary Montgomery	200	Robert Rodgers	350
John Montgomery	100	Robert Hannah	300
Elizabeth Montgomery	100	James Hannah	100
Joseph Livingston	100	Robert Stewart	100
Elizabeth Crawford	100	Richard Scott	250
Samuel Crawford	100	Philip Moore	250
John Vernor	300	John Scott	150
Robert Morrison	100	Jane Scott	100
John Metland	150	Robert Patterson	100
John Mullen	100	George Montgomery	150
James Kerr	100	Thomas Martin	100
Nath'l Hartness	250	William Martin	100
William Tagart	200	William Downes	300
William Moore	250	Edward Sminns	100

Names	Acres	Names	Acres
Elizabeth Bell	100	Hugh Morrison	300
James Lewers	100	Alexander McKelvie	100
James Lewers	100	James Sale	100
Michael Lewers	100	Robert Wilson	100
Robert Young	200	James Kerr	150
Jane Young	100	Henry Semour	100
John Young	100	John Brown	150
John Griffen	300	Patrick Dicky	100
Robert Reynolds	100	John Foster	100
Michael Roache	100	John Foster	100
James Barber	100	James Foster	100
Jane Park	100	James Waugh	100
Rachel Campbell	100	Robert Patterson	100
William McCaddam	100	David Dunn	100
Mary Martin	100	John Biggam	100
Arthur Harrison	100	Ann Higginson	100
Robert Moine	100	In or near Boonesborough or	
John Byrne	100	Belfast Township.	

The petitioners set forth that they were protestants and had lately arrived in this province on the encouragement of the Bounty given by an Act of the General Assembly of this province passed the 25th. day of July 1761 and therefore praying the same, and they having severally produced certificates as required by the said Act, It was Ordered that the Secretary do prepare Warrants of survey and that the public Treasurer do pay their Bounties to Messrs. Torrans and Pouag and Mr. Bath in consideration of their passages in the ship Nancy, Captain Hannah Commander.

Names	Ages	Names	Ages
James Robinson	42	Mary Gordon	5
Grizil Robinson	40	James Rainer	37
Thomas Robinson	13	Mary Rainer	39
George Robinson	10	James Cunningham	45
John Robinson	7	Jane Cunningham	42
Mary Jameison	20	Jane Cunningham	16
Grizil Jameison	18	John Cunningham	14
Ann Gordon	17	James Cunningham	12
Jane Gordon	13	Margaret Cunningham	8

Names	Ages	Names	Ages
Sarah Cunningham	4	Sarah McCann	8
John Cunningham	38	James McKelvy	42
Martha Cunningham	34	Margaret McKelvy	48
Joseph Cunningham	8	Alexander McKelvy	15
Margaret Cunningham	4	William McKelvy	14
John Russel	49	John McKelvy	5
Isobell Russel	47	James McKelvy	16
Martha Russel	15	Jane McKelvy	8
Ann Russel	13	Hugh McKelvy	2
James Russell	12	Robert Peacock	37
John Russell	10	Henry Peacock	14
William Hay	41	Susannah Peacock	11
Robert Hay	3	Mary Peacock	3
Elizabeth	40	Hugh Kimble	46
Samuel Knox	18	Sarah Kimble	42
James McCann	14	Abraham Kimble	10
Robert Boyd	51	Mary Kimble	7
Mary Boyd	50	John Ard	29
William Boyd	18	Jane Ard	27
Andrew Boyd	14	Mary Ard	7
Robert Boyd	9	John Ard	3
Agnes Boyd	6	John Conn	16
James McCullock	19	Matthew Reid	38
James Smith	21	Mary Reid	36
John Smith	15	Sarah Reid	5
Hugh Morrison	50	John Turk	47
Elizabeth Morrison	52	Jane Turk	47
Sarah Morrison	19	William Turk	20
Margaret Morrison	17	Jannet Turk	17
Robert Morrison	15	Ann Turk	13
Elizabeth Morrison	13	James Reid	38
Rachel Morrison	10	Ann Reid	36
Philip Bracking	39	Mary Reid	7
Ester Bracking	38	Catherine Reid	5
Richard Bracking	14	John Reid	3
Sarah Bracking	12	John Gamble	19
Henry McCann	40	Samuel Gamble	16
Jane McCann	37	James Gamble	21
William McCann	18	Martha Jordan	41

Names	Ages	Names	Ages
Jane Jordan	19	James Forster	14
Isobell Jordan	17	John Forster	12
Thomas Jordan	15	Ann Willson	38
Elizabeth Jordan	13	Robert Willson	37
Margaret Jordan	12	Walter Stewart	29
Jannet Rodgers	39	Hannah Jameison	32
Elizabeth Rodgers	11	Samuel Forster	25
Catherine Rodgers	9	George Craig	39
William Andrews	30	Mary Craig	36
Mary Andrews	31	Elizabeth Craig	17
Elizabeth Andrews	13	John Montgomery	17
David Andrews	8	Elizabeth Montgomery	15
Sarah Dicky	7	James Montgomery	12
Samuel Mark	37	George Montgomery	13
Sarah Mark	35	Mary Montgomery	50
Rose Mark	14	Joseph Livingston	16
Agnes Mark	12	Elizabeth Crawford	23
Samuel Woodside	33	Samuel Crawford	21
Jane Woodside	36	John Vernor	30
Mary Woodside	14	Mary Vernor	30
Nathaniel Boyd	29	Martha Vernor	10
Ann Boyd	27	Jane Vernor	8
Isobell Boyd	6	Robert Vernor	5
John McBirney	33	Robert Morrison	17
Margaret McBurney	31	John Metland	27
Mary McBirney	13	Marg'rt Metland	23
John McBirney	7	John Millen	21
Adam Mule	18	James Kerr	26
James Hamilton	22	Nathan Hartness	32
Francis Rodman	25	Jane Hartness	30
William Boyd	41	Jannet Hartness	8
Jane Boyd	39	David Hartness	4
Samuel Boyd	16	William Tagart	28
Mary Boyd	14	Agness Taggart	27
Jane ————	13	Agness Taggart	2
John Cox	24	William Moore	50
Ann Cox	21	Isobel Moore	51
John Duncan	29	Robert Moore	18
John Forster	32	Martha Moore	16

Names	Ages	Names	Ages
Agnes Moore	14	James McDougal	20
James Moore	12	James Develin	28
Alexander Hamilton	21	Robert Dennise	19
Agness Hamilton	20	James McMullen	18
Joseph Neilson	36	Mathew Bell	24
Grizil Neilson	31	Eleanor Bell	23
Robert Wiseman	52	James Campbell	18
Marg't Wiseman	51	William Bonnar	42
Hugh Wiseman	19	Mary Bonnar	57
Mary Wiseman	16	John Bonnar	16
Jannet Wiseman	14	James Bonnar	14
Ann Wiseman	10	Rebecca Bonnar	4
James Lawfin	32	David Lockhart	22
Mary Lawfin	31	Catherine Lockhart	19
Samuel Lawfin	16	Robert Rogers	36
William Sloan	14	Elizabeth Rogers	33
David Sloan	12	John Rogers	14
James Sloan	15	Mary Rogers	10
William Sale	38	Jane Rogers	8
Mary Sale	36	Margaret Rogers	5
James Sale	15	Robert Hannah	40
William Sale	13	Mary Hannah	41
Mary Sale	9	James Hannah	18
John Sale	6	Sophia Hannah	13
David Kennedy	36	Elias Hannah	12
Elizabeth Kennedy	32	Richard Hannah	11
John Kennedy	14	Robert Stewart	22
James Kennedy	8	Richard Scott	26
Margaret Kennedy	4	Elizabeth Scott	24
David Black	31	David Scott	5
William Black	9	Margaret Scott	4
Ester Black	12	Philip Moore	26
Sarah Black	6	Penelope Moore	28
James Johnston	37	Fanny Moore	5
Jane Johnston	35	John Scott	36
Robert Johnston	16	Agnes Scott	35
Jane Johnston	10	Jane Scott	18
Isaac Johnston	8	Robert Patterson	27
John Copeland	21	George Montgomery	24

Names	Ages	Names	Ages
Agness Montgomery	22	Isobell Griffen	27
Thomas Martin	18	Rose Griffen	12
William Martin	14	William Griffen	10
William Downs	26	Jane Griffen	8
Mary Downs	23	Robert Reynolds	21
Ann Downs	8	Michael Brooke	21
Mary Downs	5	James Barber	27
Robert Downs	3	Jane Park	16
Edward Simms	18	Downy Rogers	8
Elizabeth Bell	22	Richard Campbell	22
James Lewers	18	William McCaddam	19
Michael Lewers	16	Mary Martin	24
James Lewis	21	Arthur Harrison	22
Robert Young	39	Robert Moin	22
Mary Young	42	John Bryne	14
Jane Young	18	Ann Higginson	20
John Young	16	George Alexander	40
Agness Young	12	Elizabeth Alexander	36
John Griffen	32		

The petitioners setting forth that they were protestants and had lately arrived in this Province on the encouragement and Bounty given by the Act of the General Assembly of this Province passed the twenty fifth day of July one thousand seven hundred and sixty one and therefore praying the same and they having severally produced certificates as required by the Act, It was Ordered that the public Treasurer do pay their several Bounties to Messrs. Torrans Pouag and Bath in consideration for their passage in the ship Nancy Captain Hannah Commander.

COUNCIL JOURNAL 33, page 193-196.

Meeting of 7th. July 1767.

The following Petitions for Warrants of Survey on the Bounty were also presented and read viz

Peter Lepol	100	at or near Hillsboro Township.
John Henrick Daught	100	ditto
James Dorman	100	at or near Long Canes.
Fred'k And'w Kneider	100	at or near Hillsboro Township.

Michael Doharty	100	at or near Long Canes.
George Alexander	100	do
Thomas William Bend	100	at or near Hillsboro Township.
Ludwig Thummin	100	do

The petitioners set forth that they were protestants and had lately arrived in this Province on the encouragement and Bounty given by the Act of the General Assembly of this province passed the 25th. day of July 1761 and therefore praying the same and they having severally produced Certificates as required by the said Act

It was ORDERED that the Secretary do prepare Warrants of Survey and that the public Treasurer do pay them the Bounty as required by said Act.

Read also the petition of Sophia Schimdt the Elder and Sophia Schimdt the Younger praying to be allowed the said Bounty they having lately arrived in this province from Holland with an intention to become settlers therein

ORDERED that the Public Treasurer do pay them the Bounty agreeable to the prayers of their Petitions.

COUNCIL JOURNAL 33, pages 229-234
Meeting of 1 Sept. 1767.

The following petitions for Warrants of Survey on the Bounty were presented and read, viz:

	Acres		Acres
Mary Black	100	James Willson	350
Maria Black	100	Alexander Willson	100
Elizabeth Black	100	John Willson	100
John McClure	250	Mary Willson	100
Jane McClure	100	John Willson	100
William McClure	100	David Kensey	100
James Rowan	250	Robert Alexander	100
James Dodds	350	John Skillen	100
Andrew Barr	100	John Skillen	100
William Cooey	300	Isabella Skillen	100
Samuel Cooey	100	James Piper	100
James Doharty	350	William Rowan	150
James Doharty	100	Alexander Denhim	350
Samuel Alexander	100	Thomas Carswell	300

	Acres		Acres
Joseph Carswell	100	Francis Walker	100
Jane Carswell	100	William Walker	100
John Carswell	100	Isabella Walker	200
Robert McMinn	100	John Walker, Jun'r	300
George Knox	100	John Baron	100
Robert McCann	100	Jannet Cooey	100
Thomas Clark	250	Archibald McLaughlin	100
Charity Rankin	150	James White	450
Samuel Dodds	450	James Hogan	100
Margaret Dodds	100	Robert Brown	100
Agnes Dodds	100	Robert Brown, Sen'r	300
James Scott	300	Sarah Brown	100
James Porter	250	Mary Brown	100
James Walker	150	Roger Brown	100
James Stewart	100	John Brown	100
Edward Slacey	100	Rebekah Brown	100
Thomas Butler	200	Daniel Harshaw	100
William Kenny	100	Thomas Goucher	100
John Airs	150	Jane Lister	100
Thomas Airs	100	William Palmer	100
John Airs	100	Zachariah Champion	100
Margaret Airs	100	Thomas Smith	100
William Airs	100	Jane Hutchins	150
Susannah Airs	100	Peter Heyland	150
John Kenny	100	Robert Proctor	150
Samuel Richardson	100	David Brown	200
John Robertson	100	William Brynan	150
William Robertson	100	Robert Brynan	100
John Fortune	350	Esther Brynam	100
Mary Fortune	100	Jane Brynan	100
William Fortune	100	John Miller	150
John Fortune, Jun'r	100	John Willson	100
Robert Weir	100	John Givin	100
Andrew Morrison	200	James Reid	100
John Hall	150	Hugh Willson	100
Solomon Cunningham	100	Archibald Wyley	100
John Walker	150	William Narney	150

At or near the Long Canes on Savannah River.

ORDERED That the Secretary do prepare Warrants of Survey as prayed for by the petitioners.

COUNCIL JOURNAL 33, page 234-237.

Meeting of 1st. September 1767.

The following poor persons presented petitions to his Excellency the Governor setting forth that they were protestants and had lately arrived in this Province from Newry in the ship Britannia John Bryan Commander on the encouragement and bounty given by the Act of the General Assembly of this province passed the 25th day of July 1761 and therefore prayed the same.

Names	Ages	Names	Ages
Christian McClure	40	William Skillen	12
Jannet McClure	12	Teresa Narney	33
John McClure	7	Elizabeth Piper	26
Samuel McClure	4	Agnes Rowan	28
Isabell Rowan	28	Margaret Rowan	8
Grizil Rowan	6	Elizabeth Rowan	6
Margaret Rowan	4	Mary Rowan	2
Martha Dodds	36	Dorcas Dennin	30
Elizabeth Dodds	12	Agnes Dennin	7
John Dodds	8	Robert Dennim	5
James Dodds	4	James Dennim	3
William Dodds	2½	Ann Carswell	40
Jane Cooey	30	Thomas Carswell	14
John Cooey	13	George Carswell	12
William Cooey	12	Rebecca Carswell	7
Joseph Cooey	3	Mary Clark	6
Ann Dougharty	38	Jane Clark	5
John Dougharty	13	Elizabeth Clark	3
Daniel Dougharty	8	Jane Rankin	2
Edward Dougharty	4	Margaret Dodds	24
Margaret Willson	50	Jane Dodds	13
Isaac Willson	12	James Dodds	11
James Willson	8	Samuel Dodds	11
Samuel Willson	5	Elizabeth Dodds	8
Jane Willson	10	John Dodds	5
Margaret Skillen	48	Hannah Scott	28

Names	Ages	Names	Ages
John Scott	9	Agnes Walker	7
Mary Scott	8	Mary Walker	2
Grisil Scott	3	John Walker	4
Margaret Porter	37	Elizabeth White	35
Jane Porter	13	John White	14
James Proctor	10	Michael White	13
Margaret Walker	20	Thomas White	12
Mary Butler	22	George White	6
Ann Butler	2	William White	4
Catharine Airs	57	James White	8
John Kinny	22	Ann Brown	42
Jane Robinson	20	Mathew Brown	12
Sarah Robinson	2	William Brown	8
Ann Fortune	41	Elizabeth Brown	2
Jane Fortune	13	Agnes Hutchinson	23
Mark Fortune	12	Ann Heyland	22
Richard Fortune	9	Jane Proctor	20
Elizabeth Fortune	8	Flora Brown	25
Margaret Robinson	28	James Brynam	52
Margaret Hall	22	Agnes Miller	27
Agnes Walker	60	Robert Hutchinson	2
Elizabeth Walker	6	Margaret Walker	5
Mary Walker	31	Mary Walker	2
Isobell Walker	13		

ORDERED that the public Treasurer do pay their Bounties of four pounds and two pounds sterling according to their respective ages to Messrs Torrans & Pouag in behalf of the owners of the said ship and the remaining twenty shillings to themselves agreeable to the direction of the said Act.

COUNCIL JOURNAL 33, page 284-285.
Meeting of 24th. November 1767.

The following Petitions praying for Warrants of Survey on the Bounty were presented and read VIZ

Robert Camron	100	
Alexander Johnston	100	Acres of Land at or near the
William Begg	100	Long Canes.
James Brymer	100	

The Petitioners severally produced Certificates as required by the Act of the General Assembly passed the 25th. of July 1761 Certifying that they were respectively protestants and of good behaviour and therefore prayed to be allowed the Bounty given by the said Act which was accordingly allowed them and the Public Treasurer was Ordered to pay the Bounty of four pounds Sterling for each of them to Herculus Angus Master of the ship they came over in towards payment of their passages and the remaining Bounty of Twenty Shillings Sterling to themselves agreeable to the directions of the said Act and that the Secretary do prepare Warrants of Survey agreeable to the prayers of the Petitions.

Read also the following Petitions on the Bounty

Acres

Nathan Jones 150 at or near the Long Canes (on the Bounty)
John Peter   100   do   do
Anne Jones   100   do and the Bounty allowed
by the Act of Assembly passed 25th. July 1761.

ORDERED that the Secretary do prepare Warrants of Survey and that the Public Treasurer do pay the Bounty agreeable to the prayers of the petitioners.

COUNCIL JOURNAL 33, page 306-311.
Meeting of 12th. December 1767.

The Clerk reported to his Excellency that agreeable to his Orders he had been on Board the ship Pearl Walter Buckanan Master and had sworn the passengers lately arrived here from Scotland and Ireland agreeable to a List he delivered into the Board.

The following Petitions from the following Persons were presented and read setting forth that they were Protestants and had lately arrived from Great Britain and Ireland on the encouragement of the Bounty given by the Act of the General Assembly of this Province passed the 25th. day of July 1761 and therefore prayed the same and also Warrants for their Lands.

	Acres		Acres
Hugh McGibbon	100	Margaret Dougal	100
George Smith	100	David Hewson	100
Thomas Lowe	100	Mary Dirkie	100
Robert Reid	100	Jane Manson	100
Hugh McDougall	100	Ann Spradling	100
William Todd	100	Barbara Sutherland	100
David Duncan	100	William Taylor	100
David Mitchell	100	Daniel Prosser	100
James Smith	100	Edward Bowling	100
John Smith	100	Richard Lewis	100
Alexander Hendrick	100	Jane Jefferet	100
Patrick Smily	100	Jeremiah Simmons	100
Alexander Campbell	100	Elizabeth Chamson	100
John Arbuche	100	Ann Gilbert	100
John Stuart	100	Junian Gilbert	100
Robert Willson	100	Ann Barry	100
William McKewn	100	Mary Murry	100
Margaret Shelburne	100	Catherine Cotteral	100
Hannah Pride	100	Mary Connolly	100
Margaret Summerville	100	Honor McGrath	100
Isabell Brown	100	Elizabeth Burk	100
Jane Voice	100	Mary Dunn	100
Isabel Taylor	100	Catherine Power	100
Barbara Cooper	100	Thomas Cunningham	100

In Granville County.

ORDERED that the Secretary do prepare Warrants of Survey accordingly. And that the Public Treasurer do pay the Bounties of four pounds sterling for each of them to Henry Laurens Esq. on behalf of the owners of the ship they came over in towards payment of their passages and the remaining twenty shillings to themselves agreeable to the directions of the said Act on Mr. Laurens entering into Security to repay the Bounty he shall receive if he does not produce Certificates in favor of them as required by the said Act.

Council Journal 33, page 311.

Meeting of 15th. December 1767.

The following Petitions for Warrants of Survey on the Bounty were presented and read AND the Bounty allowed by the Act of Assembly passed the 25th. July 1761

Henry Gibson   100 acres in Granville County
Robert Spence   100 acres in Granville County

ORDERED that the Secretary do prepare Warrants of Survey accordingly and that the Clerk do issue his Certificates to the public Treasurer to pay them the Bounty agreeable to the directions of the said Act.

Council Journal 33, page 312-325.

Meeting of 22nd. December 1767.

The Clerk reported to the Board that in pursuance of His Excellency the Governor's directions he had been on board the ship Earl of Denegal Duncan Ferguson Master and had sworn the Irish passengers arrived in her to their being Protestants and having come over on the encouragement and bounty given by the Act of the General Assembly passed the 25th. day of July 1761 agreeable to a List he had delivered in at the Board Petitions praying to be allowed the said Bounty from the undermentioned persons were then presented and read

Names	Ages	Names	Ages
Andrew Simpson	25	Margaret Cahy	40
William Blakely	52	William McCullough	40
Elizabeth Blakely	54	Christian McCullough	46
Mary Blakely	4	Elizabeth McCullough	9
David Blakely	22	Patrick Spence	50
Chambers Blakly	18	Mary Spence	60
Elizabeth Blakly	28	Joseph Spence	20
Sarah Blakly	24	Robert Spence	16
Agnes Moore	20	Jannet Spence	18
Michal Willson	33	James Bell	40
Margaret Willson	23	Mary Bell	45
Charles Willson	5	James Bell Jun'r	14
Jane Willson	4	Samuel Bell	10
Adam Cahy	40	John Bell	6

Names	Ages	Names	Ages
Mary Bell	13	Isabel White	7
Elizabeth Bell	17	Jannet White	5
John Hamilton	20	Victoria White	3
John McKewn	36	James Stewart	26
Andrew McKewn	40	Rose Stewart	22
Alexander McKewn	8	Eleanor White	50
Agnes McKewn	12	Hugh Bonar	18
Mary McKewn	10	Walter Brown	30
James Spence	21	Margaret Brown	30
Sarah Spence	20	John Brown	6
John Anderson	28	Samuel Kelso	45
Elizabeth Anderson	28	Susan Kelso	44
Robert Owen	22	Jannet Kelso	16
Elizabeth Owen	20	Elizabeth Kelso	13
John McDougal	50	Isabell Kelso	12
Jannet McDougal	40	Samuel Kelso	10
Jannet McDowell	14	Margaret Kelso	8
Mary McDowell	8	John Kelso	6
Agnes McDowell	4	George Kelso	17
John McDowell	13	Samuel Willson	40
William McDowell	20	Mary Willson	38
Margaret McDowell	18	John Willson	12
James McDowell	23	Margaret Willson	8
Mary McDowell	23	Thomas Willson	4
David Usher	40	Ann Willson	10
Ann Usher	39	Elizabeth Willson	14
David Usher	15	James Wylie	45
Daniel Usher	13	Sarah Wylie	38
Ann Usher	6	Rebecca Wylie	11
John Usher	18	Margaret Wylie	9
Samuel Armstrong	25	Samuel Wylie	6
Mary Armstrong	23	John Wylie	4
William Armstrong	2	Mary McKinney	70
Margaret Armstrong	60	Dougal Ballentine	50
John White	47	Elizabeth Ballentine	50
Ann White	40	Margaret McClelan	21
William White	14	Robert Ballentine	11
Margaret White	11	William Ballentine	22
Helen White	9	Elizabeth Ballentine	17

89

Names	Ages	Names	Ages
Mary Ballentine	19	Jane Kirkpatrick	50
William Taylor	40	Robert Kirkpatrick	20
Jannet Taylor	37	John Caeson	20
Margaret Taylor	13	Hugh Caldwell	30
Jannet Taylor	5	Robert Wylie	30
Robert Taylor	10	David Spence	60
John Taylor	2	Robert Spence	12
William Taylor	17	Jannet Spence	40
Patrick Harbison	34	Martha Spence	8
Jane Harbison	22	Adam Spence	2
John Harbison	4	Agnes Spence	16
Mary Harbison	8	Francis Murphy	6
Robert Willson	51	Margaret Spence	24
Elizabeth Willson	25	Mary Spence	20
Joseph Willson	6	Eleanor Spence	17
James Willson	4	Mathew Gaston	19
Samuel Frazier	25	Peter Wylie	50
Elizabeth Frazier	25	Ann Wylie	47
Robert Robinson	60	Mary Wylie	13
Susannah Robinson	50	William Wylie	7
Waterhouse Robinson	13	Margaret Wylie	20
Alexander Hook	22	James Wylie	18
Rachel Singleton	24	Francis Wylie	17
Margaret Robinson	29	Adam Harbison	46
Jane Robinson	27	Mary Harbison	36
Thomas Robinson	22	Jannet Harbison	13
John Robinson	20	James Harbison	6
Robert Robinson	16	Elizabeth Harbison	3
Clark Hall	39	John Caldwell	60
Mary Hall	46	James Caldwell	24
Charles Hall	14	Elizabeth Caldwell	20
George Hall	11	John Andrew	36
Samuel Hall	8	Jane Andrew	36
James Hall	4	Samuel Andrew	13
Alexander Hall	18	Margaret Andrew	9
William Hall	16	Alice Andrew	6
David Spence	28	John Andrew	3
Martha Spence	24	William Andrew	2
Mary Spence	6	George Hall	26
Thomas Kirkpatrick	48	Jane Hall	27

Names	Ages	Names	Ages
William Hall	7	James Blair	9
John Hall	3	Jane Blair	2
John Walker	40	Samuel Caldwell	20
Elizabeth Walker	32	James McCartney	30
Andrew Walker	12	John McCartney	5
Thomas Walker	10	John Knox	50
Jane Walker	8	Elizabeth Knox	40
Mary Walker	5	Hugh Knox	10
James Gray	40	Sarah Knox	17
Jane Gray	40	James Knox	16
James Gray	13	William Knox	50
George Gray	10	William Boyd	20
Elizabeth Gray	7	James Crawford	20
Thomas Gray	5	David Carrol	34
Robert Gray	17	Jane Carrol	23
William Marshall	41	Mary Carrol	5
Elizabeth Marshall	39	David Dunsman	17
Robert Marshall	13	Margaret Dunsman	20
Jannet Marshall	7	Samuel Alston	26
Mary Marshall	5	Ralph McDougal	18
Jane Marshall	16	James McCleland	48
William Boyd	20	Catherine McCleland	46
Martha Boyd	17	Henry McCleland	14
John Cary	37	John McCleland	10
Mary Cary	37	Martha McCleland	8
Robert Man	40	William McCleland	3
Susannah Man	40	William Russell	42
James Man	11	Margaret Russell	44
Jannet Man	8	William Russell	14
John Man	5	Margaret Russell	10
Robert Man	3	Mary Russell	20
Arthur Cunningham	30	David Russell	18
Jane Cunningham	30	James Russell	16
Anne Cunningham	7	Adam Thomson	30
James Cunningham	4	Mary Thomson	30
James Lamont	30	John Thomson	8
Alice Lamont	20	Peter Thomson	6
John Lamont	5	Ann Thomson	4
Thomas Blair	38	Adam Thomson	2
Margaret Blair	33	William Wylie	20

ORDERED that the Public Treasurer do pay the Bounty of four pounds and two pounds sterling according to their respective ages to Messrs. Torrans and Pouag in Consideration of their passages and the remaining twenty shillings sterling to themselves agreeable to the directions of the said Act.

ORDERED that the Secretary do prepare the following Warrants of Survey on the Bounty.

	Acres		Acres
Andrew Simpson	100	Eleanor White	100
William Blakely	200	Hugh Bonar	100
David Blakely	100	Walter Brown	200
Chambers Blakely	100	Samuel Kelso	400
Elizabeth Blakely	100	Jannet Kelso	100
Sarah Blakely	100	George Kelso	100
Agnes Moore	100	Samuel Wilson	400
Michael Wilson	250	James Wylie	350
Adam McCahy	150	Mary McKinley	100
William McCullouch	250	Dougal Ballentine	100
Patrick Spence	150	William Ballentine	100
Joseph Spence	100	Margaret Ballentine	100
Robert Spence	100	Elizabeth Ballentine	100
Jannet Spence	100	William Taylor	350
James Bell	350	William Taylor	100
Elizabeth Bell	100	Patrick Harbison	200
John Hamilton	100	Mary Harbison	100
John McKewn	350	Robert Wilson	200
James Spence	150	Samuel Frazier	150
John Anderson	150	Robert Robinson	300
Robert Owen	150	Alexander Hook	100
John McDowell	350	Rachel Singleton	100
William McDowell	100	Mary Robinson	100
Margaret McDowell	100	Jane Robinson	100
James McDowell	100	Thomas Robinson	100
David Usher	300	John Robinson	100
John Usher	100	Robert Robinson, Jun'r	100
Samuel Armstrong	200	Clark Hall	350
Margaret Armstrong	100	Alexander Hall	100
John White	450	William Hall	100
John Stewart	150	David Spence	200
Elizabeth White	100	Thomas Kirkpatrick	150

	Acres		Acres
Robert Kirkpatrick	100	Sarah Knox	100
John Carson	100	James Knox	100
Hugh Caldwell	200	William Knox	100
Robert Wylie	100	William Boyd	100
David Spence	400	David Carrol	200
Agnes Spence	100	James Crawford	100
Arthur Spence	100	David Dunsman	150
Margaret Spence	100	Samuel Aston	100
Eleanor Spence	100	Ralph McDougal	100
Mathew Gaston	100	John McCleland	350
Peter Wylie	250	William Russell	250
Margaret Wylie	100	Mary Russell	100
James Wylie	100	David Russell	100
Francis Wylie	100	James Russell	100
Adam Harbison	300	Adam Thomson	100
John Caldwell	100	William Wylie	100
James Caldwell	100	Robert Vernon	100
Elizabeth Caldwell	100	Henry Glass	100
John Andrew	400	William Dunlap	100
George Hall	250	Rev'd William Knox	100
John Walker	350	Daniel Winter	100
James Gray	350	Robert McCleland	100
Robert Gray	100	Daniel Harper	100
William Marshall	300	William Rodgers	100
Jane Marshall	100	Robert Harper	200
Wm. Boyd	150	William Harper	250
John Cary	150	James Harper	100
Robert Man	350	William Harper	100
Arthur Cunningham	300	Benjamin Harper	200
James Lamont	200	William Brownlow	300
Thomas Blair	250	Andrew Hannah	100
Samuel Caldwell	100	James Brownlow	100
Jane McCartney	150	William Johnston	100
John Knox	250		

At or near Long Canes or in Craven County.

The following persons presented petitions setting forth that they were also arrived from Ireland in the said ship on the encouragement of the Bounty and therefore prayed to be allowed the same, viz:

Names	Ages	Names	Ages
Robert Vernon	20	Benjamin Harper	30
Henry Glass	30	Martha Harper	24
William Dunlap	19	William Harper	4
William Knox	24	William Brownlow	40
Daniel Winter	25	Jane Brownlow	34
Robert McCleland	19	Jane Brownlow	6
Daniel Harper	20	John Brownlow	5
William Rodgers	25	James Brownlow	2
Agnes Rodgers	20	Andrew Hannah	19
Robert Harper	25	Mary Caldwell	30
Agnes Harper	24	James Brownlow	30
John Harper	6	James Caldwell	6
William Harper	63	William Johnston	19
Margaret Harper	56		
James Harper	16	ORDERED That the public	
William Harper	18	Treasurer do pay them the	
John Harper	14	Bounty agreeable to the direc-	
Jane Harper	11	tions of the said Act.	

COUNCIL JOURNAL 34, pages 1-10
Meeting of January 5, 1768.

The Clerk reported that he had in pursuance of his Excellency the Governors directions been on board the Brigantine Chichester William Reed Master from Belfast and administered the oaths to such of the poor protestants as were of age who lately arrived in her in this Province on the encouragement of the Bounty given by the Act of the General Assembly passed the 25th July 1761 agreeable to the following List viz't

Names	Ages	Names	Ages
Andrew Moor	18	John McFarlin	9
Simon Cameron	27	Mary McFarlin	7
John Steil	28	Robert Dickey	31
Martin Mahaffy	40	Susannah Dickey	33
Mary Mahaffy	5	William Dickey	7
Martha Mahaffy	27	James Dickey	6
Thomas Fargar	24	Elizabeth Dickey	4
Margaret Fargar	31	Jane Dickey	3
James Fargar	3	Hector Dickey	23

Names	Ages	Names	Ages
John Bell	19	Izrael Moor	24
Sarah Bell	48	Richard Moor	18
Sarah Bell	21	John Moor	9
William Johnston	17	Elizabeth Moor	20
James Kennedy	21	Jane Moor	16
Francis Hodge	29	Christopher Moor	14
Elizabeth Hodge	28	Ann Moor	12
Robert Hodge	8	Elnor Moor	5
Alexander Hodge	6	Arthur McCrachen	40
John Hodge	4	Ruth McCrachen	38
Thomas Loggan	36	Mary McCrachen	17
Mary Loggan	29	Jane McCrachen	16
John Loggan	9	William McCrachen	14
William Loggan	5	Thomas McCrachen	13
Andrew Magelton	55	Margaret McCrachen	11
Elizabeth Magelton	50	Arthur McCrachen	9
Vance Magelton	17	Samuel McCrachen	7
James Magelton	10	Ruth McCrachen	5
Peter Magelton	13	John McCrachen	3
James Henning	17	James McCrachen	1
John Hillary	15	John Boyde	25
Simon Powlson	29	Nancy Boyde	20
Mary Powlson	30	Hugh Donalson	28
Rose Powlson	2	Mary Donalson	23
John Hathorn	53	Hugh Carson	40
Elizabeth Hathorn	44	Margaret Carson	44
Adam Hathorn	22	Jane Carson	21
James Hathorn	20	Margaret Carson	19
John Hathorn	17	Jannet Carson	17
Mary Hathorn	16	Mary Carson	15
Robert Hathorn	14	Elizabeth Carson	12
Joseph Hathorn	12	William Carson	9
Benjamin Hathorn	7	Hugh Carson	7
Elizabeth Hathorn	3	James Carson	4
Robert Lowey	18	James Moorhead	58
James Loury	16	Rose Moorhead	24
Izrael Moor	55	Jane Moorhead	57
Nancy Moor	50	Prudence Moorhead	13
William Moor	27	James Moorhead	5

Names	Ages	Names	Ages
Thomas Wylie	55	John Bell	17
Jane Wylie	47	William Bell	16
Elizabeth Wylie	19	Mary Bell	5
Henry Wylie	18	James Carson	18
Thomas Wylie	16	James McCrachen	10
Jane Wylie	16	James Moorhead	17
Ann Wylie	9	John Mannary	22
Margaret Wylie	7	William Proctor	50
David Smith	23	Elizabeth Proctor	50
Robert Proctor	56	William Proctor	17
Mary Proctor	56	John Proctor	13
James Proctor	26	Samuel Proctor	12
Rose Proctor	19	James McClean	19
Mary Proctor	16	Thomas Beard	25
Margaret Proctor	13	Nancy Beard	24
Samuel Proctor	54	Mary Beard	4
Catherine Proctor	44	Martha Beard	3
Sarah Proctor	18	Robert Steil	48
Samuel Proctor	16	Margaret Steil	38
Catherine Proctor	14	James Steil	7
Philip Proctor	12	Henry Steil	4
Edward Proctor	10	Nelly Steil	13
Mary Proctor	1	Elizabeth Steil	3
William Bell	41	Elizabeth Dennise	75
Isabell Bell	40	Jane Dickey	58
Elizabeth Bell	20		

ORDERED that the public Treasurer do pay the Bounty of four pounds sterling and two pounds sterling according to their respective ages to Messrs Torrans and Pouag in Consideration of their passages and the remaining Twenty Shillings Sterling to themselves agreeable to the directions of the said Act.

The following Petitions for Warrants of Survey on the Bounty were read

	Acres		Acres
John Cameron	100	John McFarlin	150
John Steil	100	Robert Dickey	350
Martin Mahaffy	200	Hector Dickey	100
Thomas Fargar	200	John Bell	100

	Acres		Acres
Sarah Bell	100	James Moorhead	250
Sarah Bell	100	Rose Moorhead	100
William Johnston	100	Thomas Wylie	250
James Kennedy	100	Elizabeth Wylie	100
Sarah Nesbitt	100	Henry Wylie	100
Francis Hodge	300	Thomas Wylie	100
Thomas Loggan	250	Jane Wylie	100
Andrew Magelton	200	David Smith	100
Elizabeth Magelton	100	Robert Proctor	200
Vance Magelton	100	James Procter	100
James Magelton	100	Rose Procter	100
James Kenning	100	Mary Procter	100
Andrew Moor	100	Samuel Procter	350
John Hillary	100	Sarah Procter	100
Simon Powlson	200	Samuel Procter	100
James Gray	450	William Bell	200
John Hathorn	350	Elizabeth Bell	100
Adam Hathorn	100	John Bell	100
James Hathorn	100	William Bell	100
John Hathorn	100	James Carson	100
Mary Hathorn	100	James McCrachen	100
Robert Lowry	100	Arthur McCrachen	100
James Lowry	100	James Moorhead	100
Izrael Moor	350	John Mannary	100
William Moor	100	William Procter	250
Izrael Moor	100	William Procter	100
Richard Moor	100	James McClean	100
Elizabeth Moor	100	Thomas Beard	250
Jane Moor	100	Robert Steil	350
Arthur McCrachen	550	Elizabeth Dennise	100
Mary McCrachen	100	John Finley	450
Jane McCrachen	100	Jane Dickey	100
John Boyle	150		
Hugh Donaldson	150	In Granville County or Craven
Hugh Carson	350	County.
Jane Carson	100	ORDERED that the Secretary
Margaret Carson	100	do prepare Warrants of Sur-
Jannet Carson	100	vey agreeable to the prayers of
Mary Carson	100	the petitioners.

Council Journal 34, pages 9-14
Meeting of January 5, 1768.

The Clerk also reported that he had in pursuance of his Excellency the Governors directions been on board the ship Admiral Hawk John McAdam Master who had lately arrived in this Province from Londonderry with poor Irish protestants on the encouragement of the Bounty given by the Act of the General Assembly passed the 25th July 1761 and had administered the usual oaths to such as were of age, agreeable to the following list—

Names	Ages	Names	Ages
Barnabas Quin	22	Ann Wier	56
Thomas Smith	39	Benjamin Cockran	20
Mary Smith	32	John Walker	23
Nancy Smith	13	Robert Osborn	23
William Smith	8	William Brawlie	35
Samuel Smith	2	Margaret Brawlie	45
Mary Smith	1	Ann Brawlie	12
Samuel Smith	38	Thomas Brawlie	10
Sarah Smith	28	William Brawlie	7
Jane Smith	8	Ann Brawlie	58
William Smith	6	James McGown	21
Samuel Smith	4	Charles Moorhead	22
Thomas Johnston	25	Oliver Deal	23
Mary Johnston	22	William Gordon	21
Robert Spear	24	James Elweany	55
John Brown	18	William Gaston	19
William Brown	16	John Murdie	21
James Gellaspie	22	Thomas Burnside	22
James Galberth	21	James McCullouch	23
James Dafter	28	Agnes McCullouch	20
Mary Dafter	2	Hannah Lindsey	19
Margaret Dafter	28	James Summerville	23
Margaret Peopler	40	John Bell	35
Mary Peopler	11	Martha Bell	35
Martha Peopler	13	John Bell	6
Elizabeth Peoplar	8	Jane Bell	12
John Peoplar	4	Alexander Bell	3
William Douglass	19	William Bean	40

Names	Ages	Names	Ages
Nomiah Bean	30	Mary Davis	9
William Bean	13	Elizabeth Davis	5
Thomas Bean	3	Patrick McDougal	30
Hannah Flint	33	Annias McDougal	25
Elizabeth Flint	13	Dougal McDougal	56
John Flint	6	Elnor McDougal	54
John Shaw	30	Alexander McDougal	21
William Watt	28	Mary McDougal	26
Isabell Watt	50	Jane Watt	39
William McMorris	32	John Watt	36
Jane McMorris	32	Izabell Watt	2
Mary McMorris	10	Christopher Watt	8
William McMorris	8	William Watt	11
Ann McMorris	6	Mary Watts	14
Jane McMorris	4	Ann Watts	13
James McMorris	1	Orley Watts	6
James Davis	30	John Watt	4
Elizabeth Davis	30		

ORDERED that the public Treasurer do pay the Bounties of four pounds and two pounds sterling according to their respective ages to Messrs Torrans and Pouag in Consideration of their passages and the remaining Twenty Shillings Sterling to themselves agreeable to the directions of the said Act.

The following Petitions for Warrants of Survey on the Bounty were presented and read VIZ—

	Acres		Acres
Barnabas Quin	100	Ann Wier	100
Thomas Smith	350	Benjamin Cockran	100
Samuel Smith	300	John Walker	100
Thomas Johnston	150	Robert Osborn	100
Robert Spear	100	William Brawlie	300
John Brown	100	Ann Brawlie	100
William Brown	100	James McGown	100
James Gellespie	100	Charles Moorhead	100
James Galbreth	100	Oliver Deal	100
John Drafter	200	James Gordon	100
Margaret Peopler	300	James Elweany	100
William Douglass	100	William Alston	100

Names	Acres	Names	Acres
John Murdie	100	Patrick McDougal	100
Thomas Burnside	100	Annias McDougal	100
James McCullouch	150	Dougal McDougall	150
Hannah Lindsey	100	Alexander McDougal	100
James Summerville	100	Mary McDougal	100
John Bell	100	John Watt	500
Martha Bell	250	In Granville or Craven Coun-	
William Bean	250	ty.	
Hannah Flint	200	ORDERED that the Secre-	
John Shaw	100	tary do prepare Warrants of	
William McMorris	400	Survey agreeable to the pray-	
James Davies	300	ers of the respective Petitions.	

COUNCIL JOURNAL 34, pages 24-33
Meeting of January 12, 1768.

The Clerk reported that he had in pursuance of his Excellency the Governors directions been on board the snow James and Mary John Moore Master from Larne and administered the oaths to such of the poor protestants as were of age who had lately arrived in her into this Province on the encouragement and Bounty given by an Act of the General Assembly of this Province passed the 25th July 1761 agreeable to the following list

Names	Ages	Names	Ages
Alexander Tomb	27	Mary Beaty	19
Elizabeth Tomb	25	John Beaty	17
David Tomb	5	Jane Beaty	13
John Cabin	16	David McCally	16
John Fillips	34	John Morton	39
Jane Fillips	34	Jane Morton	26
Robert Fillips	13	David Morton	7
Jane Fillips	5	John Morton	4
Mary Fillips	10	Elizabeth Morton	2
John Fillips	7	Thomas Peadin	24
Elizabeth Fillips	2½	Robert Simpton	46
Robert Fillips	20	Margaret Simpton	39
Robert Beaty	48	Mary Simpton	14
Jane Beaty	50	Sarah Simpton	11

Names	Ages	Names	Ages
John Simpton	5	Alexander Davidson	48
Elizabeth Beally	45	Jannet Davidson	36
Edward Beally	28	Samuel Glegney	30
James Willson	4	Mary Glegney	28
Margaret Willson	46	Joseph Glegney	21
William Willson	22	Agnes Taylor	35
Ann Willson	20	William Taylor	12
John Willson	17	Margaret Taylor	10
James Willson	16	Samuel Taylor	44
Jane Willson	12	Mathew Gelespy	23
Thomas Patterson	19	Martha Gelespy	26
Samuel Young	29	Alexander Kanny	34
James Fleming	42	Margaret Kanny	36
Mary Fleming	45	Agnes Kanny	8
Alexander Fleming	16	Isabell Kanny	4
John Fleming	14	Mary Watson	17
Margaret Campbell	59	Robert Rowan	55
James Martin	38	Sarah Rowan	35
Jane Martin	39	William Rowan	7½
William Martin	13	Jane Rowan	69
John Martin	12	John Crawford	24
Jane Martin	10	William Scott	40
Andrew Martin	8	Mary Scott	35
James Martin	6	James Scott	14
Hugh Young	35	William Scott	10
Margaret Young	35	Robert Scott	7
Sarah Young	15	Ann Scott	8
Elizabeth Young	13	John Scott	4
Agnes Young	10	Thomas Crossan	46
James Young	7	Jane Crossan	46
Jane Young	19	Thomas Crossan	20
James Nichol	30	Agnes Crossan	17
Elizabeth Nichol	28	Jane Crossan	18
Margaret Nichol	7	Helen Crossan	11
Sarah Nichol	4	John Crossan	5
Daniel McCoy	26	Christian McALeas	46
James Paul	29	John McAleas	23
Agnes Paul	4	Daniel McALeas	17
William Paul	3	Ann McALeas	11

Names	Ages	Names	Ages
Hugh McALeas	8	William Paull	2
Andrew Owens	39	John Reed	33
Jane Owens	39	Agnes Reed	26
Robert Owens	17	James Reed	4
James Owens	13	William Reed	2
Jane Owens	10	Patrick Hamilton	32
Elizabeth Owens	6	Nelly Hamilton	34
James Dunsheth	27	Jenny Hamilton	5
Mary Dunsheth	31	Mary Hamilton	4
William Dunsheth	2	Elizabeth Wallace	47
Henry McCallaster	20	Martha Wallace	17
James Corry	43	Robert Wallace	16
George Corry	16	Agnes Wallace	13
John Corry	7	William Farris	21
William Turner	50	Mary Farris	26
Margaret Turner	57	Jane Dunn	50
Alexander Turner	20	Agnes Dunn	18
John Turner	16	James Dunn	16
James Turner	12	William Caldwell	26
Thomas McWhirter	19	Elizabeth Caldwell	26
Mary Smith	49	Martha Caldwell	6
Robert Miller	40	Jannet Caldwell	4
John Bouys	20	Elizabeth Caldwell	23
Nancy Gordon	25	Mary Caldwell	53
Alexander Gordon	7	Martha Caldwell	21
Charles McClinto	26	Moses Caldwell	20
Mary McClinto	38	Mary Caldwell	17
Joseph McClinto	6	James Douglass	34
Nath'l McClinto	4	Rose Douglas	32
Patrick McGill	38	Mary Douglass	8
Elizabeth McGill	38	Robert Douglass	11
William McGill	12	James Douglass	4
Mary McGill	8	James Douglass	40
Richard McGill	4	Agness Douglass	50
Archibald Paull	36	Mary Douglass	16
Agnes Paull	34	Alexander Douglass	14
James Paull	10	Isabell Douglass	12
Sarah Paull	8	Arew McCleland	20
Elizabeth Paull	6	Easter McCleland	20
Martha Paull	4		

ORDERED that the public Treasurer do pay the Bounty of four pounds and two pounds sterling according to their respective ages to Messrs. Torrans and Pouag in consideration of their passages and the remaining twenty shillings to themselves agreeable to the directions of the said Act.

The following Petitions for Warrants of Survey on the Bounty were read, viz.

	Acres		Acres
Alexander Tomb	250	Joseph Glegney	100
John Caben	100	Samuel Taylor	250
John Fillips	400	Mathew Gilespy	150
Robert Fillips	100	Alexander Kanny	250
Robert Beaty	200	Mary Watson	100
Mary Beaty	100	Robert Rowan	200
John Beaty	100	John Crawford	100
David McCally	100	William Scott	450
John Morton	300	Thomas Crossan	300
Thomas Peadon	100	Thomas Crossan	100
Robert Simipton	300	Agnes Crossan	100
Elizabeth Beally	100	Christian McALeas	100
Edward Beally	100	John McALeas	100
James Willson	200	Daniel McALeas	100
William Willson	100	Marg't McAleas	100
Agnes Willson	100	Andrew Owens	300
John Willson	100	Robert Owens	100
James Willson	100	James Dunsheth	200
Thomas Patterson	100	Mary McCallaster	100
Samuel Young	100	Jane Corry	150
James Fleming	200	George Corry	100
Alexander Fleming	100	William Turner	200
Margaret Campbell	100	Alexander Turner	100
James Martin	400	John Turner	100
Hugh Young	300	Thomas McWhirter	100
Sarah Young	100	Mary Smith	100
Jane Young	100	Robert Miller	100
James Nichols	250	John Bouys	100
Daniel McCoy	100	Mary Gordon	150
James Paull	200	Charles McClinto	250
Alexander Davidson	150	Patrick McGill	300
Samuel Glegney	150	Archibald Paull	400

	Acres		Acres
John Reed	250	James Douglass	300
Patrick Hamilton	300	Mary Douglass	100
Elizabeth Wallace	150	Andrew McCleland	150
Martha Wallace	100	John Waugh	100
Robert Wallace	100	Jane Rowan	100
William Farris	200	Moses Caldwell	100
James Dunn	100	Mary Caldwell	100
Agnes Dunn	100		
James Dunn	100	ORDERED that the Secretary
William Caldwell	300	do prepare Warrants of Sur-
Mary Caldwell	100	vey as prayed for by the peti-
Martha Caldwell	100	tioners.

Council Journal 34, pages 53-61.
Meeting of 13th. February 1768.

Read the following Petition on the Bounty

Alexander Forgie 100 acres in Granville or Craven County and the Bounty allowed by the Act of the General Assembly of this province passed the 25th July 1761.

ORDERED that the Secretary do prepare a Warrant of Survey and that the Public Treasurer do pay him the Bounty agreeable to the directions of the said Act.

Read the following petitions for Warrants of Survey on the Bounty.

	Acres		Acres
Thomas Snead	300	John O'Neal	100
James Snead	100	Jane O'Neal	100
Mary Snead	100	James Boden	200
John Snead	100	Margaret Boden	100
Robert Snead	100	William Legg	100
Thomas Snead	100	James Fleming	150
John Waight	250	William Fleming	100
John Waight	100	Henry Green	150
Samuel Waight	100	Robert Thomson	300
Sarah Waight	100	Samuel Nelly	150
Ezekiel Townshend	100	William Nelly	300
George Lester	100	Sarah Nelly	100

	Acres		Acres
Mary Levis	100	Isabella Bailey	100
Alex'dr Brannan	150	Ann Bailey	100
John Glenn	200	William Bailey	100
William Moore	300	Hamilton Murdock	350
James McKewn	150	Andrew English	150
James Wallace	300	Penelope McClune	100
Jane Wallace	100	Peter McDowell	300
William Wallace	100	Thomas Martin	150
Mary Wallace	100	John Kinnard	350
Robert McKewn	150	John Long	100
William McKewn	100	Daniel McLean	300
James Graham	150	James McLean	100
Jonathan Read	150	Lettice McLean	100
Nathan Nichols	100	Charles Dunbar	100
John Clennending	100	John Robins	200
John Brownlie	150	John Johnston	350
Joseph Brownlie	100	Thomas McAdory	250
Ann Brownlie	100	William Meglamery	150
James Brownlie	200	Peter Waters	350
Jane Brownlie	100	Samuel Cathcart	100
Alice Brownlie	100	James Dezill	100
Nathaniel Bailey	250	Robert Beaty	100
Jannet Bailey	100	Thomas Bell	250
Joseph Bailey	100	Robert Bell	100
Elizabeth Bailey	100	John Waite	200

In Granville or Craven County.

ORDERED that the Secretary do prepare Warrants of Survey accordingly.

The following persons presented petitions to his Excellency the Governor setting forth that they were protestants and arrived in this province in the Brig Lord Dunagannon Robert Montgomery Master on the encouragement and Bounty given by the Act of the General Assembly of this Province passed the 25th July 1761 and therefore prayed to be allowed the same.

That the prayers of their petitions were granted and the public Treasurer was ordered to pay the Bountys of four pounds and two pounds sterling according to their respective ages in consideration of their passages to this Province to Messrs Torrans and Pouag in behalf of the owners of the said Brig and the remaining twenty shillings sterling to themselves agreeable to the directions of the said Act.

Names	Ages	Names	Ages
John O'Neal	40	Ann Moore	24
Margaret O'Neal	35	Elizabeth Moore	7
Jane O'Neal	15	Thomas Moore	5
Alice O'Neal	12	Robert Moore	2
Margaret O'Neal	5	James McKewn	23
Arthur O'Neal	3	Elizabeth McKewn	24
James Boden	50	James Wallace	45
Jane Bodeñ	36	Eleanor Wallace	42
Margaret Boden	18	Jane Wallace	22
Sarah Boden	2	William Wallace	18
William Leg	20	Mary Wallace	16
James Fleming	30	Robert Wallace	14
Hannah Fleming	24	Margaret Wallace	12
William Fleming	23	Elizabeth Wallace	6
Henry Green	24	Robert McKewn	52
Jane Green	22	Jane McKewn	45
Robert Thomson	40	William McKewn	17
Jane Thomson	30	James Graham	34
Sarah Thomson	9	Margaret Graham	28
William Thomson	7	Jonathan Reed	30
Andrew Thomson	3	Jane Reed	26
Samuel Nelly	45	Nathaniel Nickels	24
Jane Nelly	40	John Clenningding	21
William Nelly	32	John Browlee	40
Sarah Nelly	30	Alice Brownlee	36
Mary Nelly	15	Joseph Browlee	19
Jane Nelly	13	Ann Brownlee	15
Sarah Nelly	7	James Brownlee	32
John Nelly	4	Jane Brownlee	18
Alexander Brannan	20	Alice Brownlee	15
Mary Brannan	20	George Brownlee	11
John Glen	40	John Brownlee	8
Rose Glen	30	Nathaniel Bailey	50
Jane Glen	3	Jane Bailey	45
William Moore	36	Janet Bailey	23

Names	Ages	Names	Ages
Joseph Bailey	20	Mary McLean	8
Elizabeth Bailey	18	Charles Dunbar	24
Isabell Bailey	17	John Robins	30
Ann Bailey	16	Jane Robins	26
William Bailey	15	Isabell Robins	6
James Bailey	8	John Johnston	40
Nathaniel Bailey	6	Elizabeth Johnston	32
Hamilton Murdock	32	Catherine Johnston	8
Mary Murdock	30	Mary Johnston	6
Margaret Murdock	12.	James Johnston	4
Elizabeth Murdock	10	Jane Johnston	3
William Murdock	8	Thomas Adory	30
Jane Murdock	5	Ann Adory	26
Andrew English	26	Elizabeth Adory	6
Jane English	24	Martha Adory	4
Penelope McClune	40	William Meglamery	32
Peter McDowal	36	Hannah Meglamery	28
Jannet McDowal	34	Peter Waters	38
Thomas McDowal	7	Mary Waters	30
Margaret McDowal	6	Elizabeth Waters	14
Mary McDowal	3	Rachell Waters	8
Thomas Martin	28	David Waters	6
John Kinnard	34	Sarah Waters	3
Mary Kinnard	30	Samuel Cathcart	23
Jannet Kinnard	10	James Dezill	22
Elizabeth Kinnard	8	Robert Beaty	23
John Kinnard	5	Thomas Bell	26
William Kinnard	3	Jane Bell	33
John Long	19	Robert Bell	15
Daniel McLean	42	William Bell	13
Ann McLean	40	Thomas Bell	7
James McLean	20	John Waite	24
Lettice McLean	16	Mary Waite	23
Elizabeth McLean	14	Eleanor Waite	2
Ann McLean	11		

The following persons also presented petitions to his Excellency setting forth that they were protestants and arrived in this Province from Bristol in the ship St. Helena George Arthur Master on the encouragement and bounty given by this province passed the 25th. July 1761 and therefore humbly praying to be allowed the same.

	Ages		Ages
Thomas Snead	48	Elizabeth Snead	10
Elizabeth Snead	46	John Waight	60
Thomas Snead	24	Mary Waight	52
James Snead	23	John Waight	19
Mary Snead	21	Samuel Waight	15
John Snead	19	Benjamin Waight	13
Robert Snead	16	Sarah Waight	8
Ann Snead	13	Ezekiel Townsend	22
Richard Snead	13	George Lester	22

ORDERED that the public Treasurer do pay the Bounty of four pounds and two pounds Sterling according to their respective ages to Messrs English & Lloyd in Consideration of their passage to this province and the remaining twenty shillings sterling to themselves agreeable to the directions of the said Act.

COUNCIL JOURNAL 34, page 70-78.

Meeting of 23rd February 1768.

The following Petitions for Warrants of Survey on the Bounty were presented and read.

	Acres		Acres
Robert Potts	200	Margaret Beatty	150
John Potts	100	Agnes Beatty	100
Elizabeth Potts	100	John Henery	350
Samuel Brawford	450	Alexander Henry	100
Alexander Archer	350	Agnes Henry	100
Thomas Hill	200	William Conor	200
Samuel Hill	100	James Turner	200
Susannah Hill	100	Robert Gibson	150
Margaret Counney	150	Archibald Murry	100
John Brown	200	William Murry	100
Henry Brown	150	Robert Kennedy	100
Jane Brown	100	John Kennedy	100
Samuel Brown	100	Margaret Kennedy	100
Jane Agey	100	Eleanor Kennedy	100

	Acres		Acres
John Summers	400	Robert Biggam	200
Andrew Lethem	400	Mary Biggam	100
John Gilmore	100	Robert Biggam	100
Richard Latham	100	James Biggam	100
Margaret Gilmore	100	Margaret Biggam	100
Charles Gilmore	100	Robert Berry	150
John Gracey	200	Ann Berry	100
James Hannah	100	Robert Berry	100
Alexander Luke	100	Richard Berry	100
James Blankheed	100	James Berry	100
Joseph Nesbit	100	Mary Proctor	150
Alexander McNeight	100	Robert Hinton	250
Mary Johnston	150	James McWhar	100
Andrew Rea	350	Robert Huggins	100
Patrick Rea	100	Michael McIlrawth	100
Patrick Carson	450	Andrew Dixon	100
Thomas McCaddam	200	Oliver Dunbar	100
Rose McCaddam	100	Oliver McCashler	100
Henry McCaddam	100	Patrick McFadding	300
John Gordon	100	John Thomson	100
Alexd'r Potts	100	Samuel McConnoll	200
John Robinson	100	Agnes Willson	100
Patrick Burns	100	James Keas	100
Robert Ellis	300	John Steenson	100
Ann Ellis	100	Arthur McQueenling	100
William Ellis	100	Joseph Waid	100
Margaret Ellis	100	Jeremiah Nesbitt	100

In Berkley, Craven or Granville Countys.

ORDERED that the Secretary do prepare Warrants of Survey accordingly.

The following persons presented petitions to his Excellency setting forth that they were protestants and had arrived in this province from Ireland in the snow Gregg John Monford Master on the encouragement and Bounty given by an Act of the General Assembly passed the 25th July 1761 that the prayers of their petitions were granted and the public Treasurer was ordered to pay their Bounties of four pounds and two pounds sterling according to their respective ages in consideration of their passages to this province to Messrs Torrans and Pouag in behalf of the owners of the said snow and the remaining twenty shillings sterling to themselves agreeable to the directions of the said act.

Names	Ages	Names	Ages
Alexander Archer	27	Isabell Gibson	24
Jane Archer	25	Archibald Murry	40
Susannah Archer	6	Arthur Murry	40
Ann Archer	4	John Murry	17
William Archer	2	William Murry	15
Thomas Hill	50	Mary Murry	12
Margaret Hill	50	Agnes Murry	10
Samuel Hill	25	Jane Murry	6
Susannah Hill	16	Archibald Murry	5
William Hill	7	Robert Kennedy	56
Margaret Counney	25	John Kennedy	28
Margaret Couney	3	Margaret Kennedy	29
John Brown	32	Elizabeth Kennedy	19
Mary Brown	31	John Summers	36
John Brown	4	Agnes Summers	37
Henry Brown	25	George Summers	12
Margaret Brown	27	John Summers	10
Jane Brown	16	Ann Summers	8
Samuel Brown	15	Margaret Summers	5
Jane Agey	17	William Summers	4
Margaret Beatty	37	Andrew Lethem	38
Agnes Beatty	17	Jane Lethem	40
Elizabeth Beatty	10	John Gilmore	24
John Henery	50	Richard Lethem	16
Alexander Henery	20	Moses Lethem	14
John Hennery	14	Andrew Lethem	12
Elizabeth Hennery	40	Robert Lethem	7
Agnes Henery	16	Sarah Lethem	5
Elizabeth Henery	10	Margaret Gilmor	18
Hugh Henery	4	Charles Gilmore	15
William Conor	24	John Gracey	25
Mary Conor	26	Elizabeth Gracey	21
James Turner	30	James Hannah	24
Susannah Turner	19	Andrew Luke	20
Susannah Turner	2	James Bankheed	20
Robert Gibson	30	Joseph Nesbitt	20

Names	Ages	Names	Ages
Alexander McNight	20	Mary Biggam	20
Mary Johnston	24	Robert Biggam	20
Agnes Johnston	5	James Biggam	17
Andrew Rea	38	Joseph Biggam	7
Ester Rea	37	Margaret Biggam	15
Patrick Rea	16	Hugh Biggam	2
Archibald Rea	14	Robert Berry	50
Margaret Rea	12	Jane Berry	47
Andrew Rea	9	Ann Berry	21
John Rea	6	Robert Berry	18
Elizabeth Rea	4	Richard Berry	16
Patrick Carson	37	James Berry	15
Rebecca Carson	33	Mary Procter	23
John Carson	14	Robert Hinton	25
Catherine Carson	12	Eleanor Hinton	24
Mary Carson	11	Hannah Hinton	3
Agnes Carson	6	James McWhur	21
James Carson	3	Robert Huggins	17
Thomas McCaddam	40	Michal McIlraw	21
Catherine McCaddam	38	Oliver Dunbar	22
Rose McCaddam	20	Oliver McCashler	19
Robert McCaddam	13	Patrick McFadding	34
Henry McCaddam	18	Zuphana McFadding	42
John Gordon	21	Catherine McFadding	13
Alexander Potts	27	Mary McFadding	11
John Robinson	20	Agnes McFadding	2
Patrick Burns	24	John Thomson	27
Robert Ellis	50	Samuel McConnell	30
Ann Ellis	21	Mary McConnell	28
Esther Ellis	52	Mary McConnell	8
William Ellis	18	Agnes Willson	14
Margaret Ellis	15	Jane Keas	19
Mary Ellis	13	John Steenson	26
Joseph Ellis	12	Arthur McQueenling	24
Sarah Ellis	9	Joseph Waid	46
Robert Biggam	52	Jeremiah Nesbit	16

The following persons presented petitions to His Excellency the Governor setting forth that they were protestants and arrived in this province from Ireland in the snow Betty Gregg

John Monford Commander on the encouragement and Bounty given by the Act of the General Assembly of this Province passed the 25th July 1761 and therefore humbly prayed the same, that the prayers of their petitions were granted and the public Treasurer was Ordered to pay them the Bounty agreeable to the directions of the said Act they having paid their passages.

	Age		Age
Robert Potts	58	Jane Brawford	38
Sarah Potts	57	William Brawford	12
John Potts	21	Margaret Brawford	18
Elizabeth Potts	15	Thomas Brawford	8
Robert Potts	14	Elizabeth Brawford	6
Samuel Brawford	38	Samuel Brawford	2

COUNCIL JOURNAL 34, page 101-103.
Meeting of 9th. March 1768.

His Excellency the Governor informed the Board that Monsieur Dumese De St Pierre a french Gentleman having presented to him a Memorial to him setting forth that he sailed from Great Britain with an Intention of going to Halifax with a number of Protestant Colonists but they have been drove into this port by distress of Weather he had determined to remain here and settle in this province which Memorial His Excellency had referred to the Commons House of Assembly who had thereupon resolved to allow to them the Bounty given by the Act of the General Assembly to protestants coming from Europe to settle in this Province and the said persons attending and having taken the oaths of allegiance His Excellency was pleased to direct that the Public Treasurer should out of any money in his Hands belonging to the public pay to the said Dumesne De. St. Pierre the sum of One Thousand One Hundred and Ninety Seven Pounds Currency the sum resolved by the Assembly to be granted to them by the said Resolution.

The following petitions for Warrants of Survey on on the
Bounty were then presented and read VIZ

	Acres		Acres
Adam De Martile	100	Peter Michl. King	200
Laurens Revere	100	John Due Depré	100
Abraham Paw	150	Ann Hughes	100
Jacob Dilli Chaux	250	Henrick Gasper	100
John James Steifel	100	Robert Rogers	100
Johannes Gerlogh Flick	250	Thomas Goguett	100
Hendrick Dryer	200	Francis La. Landé	100
Ann Dorothea Elizabeth		James Sezor Boulonge	100
Yeason	100	Francis Kellet	100
Robert Castle	150	Magdeline LeQue	150
John Duvall	100	Jean Louis Demesne De	
Elizabeth Forrester	100	St. Pierre	150
Archibald Heynard	100		

In Hillsborough Township or on Savanna River

ORDERED that the Secretary do prepare Warrants of Survey as prayed for by the petitioners.

COUNCIL JOURNAL 34, page 148-151.

Meeting of 30th. May 1768.

The following Petitions for Warrants of Survey on the Bounty were presented and read VIZ

	Acres	
George Farquar	100	
Charles Tais	100	
Patrick Smellie	100	
John Grelling	100	
Robert Briggs	100	
William Weer	100	Between Savannah
John Mathews	100	and Saludy Rivers.
Stephen Brown	100	
James Stedman	100	
Gilbert Chalmers	100	
John Allardice	100	
George Thomson	100	

The following petitioners setting forth that they were protestants and had arrived in this Province from Great Britain in the Snow Kinnoul Alexander Alexander Master on the encouragement of the bounty given by this province and therefore humbly prayed to be allowed the same that the prayer of their petitions were granted and the Public Treasurer was Ordered to pay the Bounty of four pounds sterling to Alexander Alexander on behalf of the owners of the said ship and the remaining Twenty Shillings Sterling to themselves agreeable to the directions of the said Act.

George Farquer	Patrick Smellie
Charles Tais	John Grelling

114

Robert Briggs   John Allardice
Stephen Brown   George Thomson
James Stedman   William Weir
Gilbert Chamers

Council Journal 34, page 175-176.
Meeting 8th. July 1768.

The following Petitions on the Bounty for Town and Vine-
uard Lotts in Hillsborough Township were presented and read
VIZ—

Henry Marqué

John George Flick

Henry Drayer

Abram Ranald

Henry Gasperd

John Ledue desprez

Francis Heller

Cezar Boulonge   Four Acres for a Vineyard
                                  Lott In Hillsborough Township
Francis Delalande   and half an acre in New
                                  Bourdeaux for a Town Lott.
Peter Mich'l LeRoy

John Duval

Jacob Delacheau

John Jacob Stiffell

Abraham Paux

Robert Rogers

Laurens Revierre

COUNCIL JOURNAL 34, page 176.
Meeting of 8th. July 1768.

His Honor the Lieutenant Governor observed to the Board that the Act giving the Bounty would expire with a prorogation of the Assembly and as it had appeared of late that several people had petitioned for it who were no ways intitled to it and as no persons could be expected now from Europe who would come really and bona fide on encouragement given by it and therefore desired the opinion of the Board if it might not be proper by Proroguering the Assembly to put an end to it. And the Board Concurring in opinion with him his Honor by their advice directed the Secretary to prepare a Proclamation proroguing the Assembly to Tuesday the 13th day of September next.

COUNCIL JOURNAL 34, page 249.
Meeting of 15th. Sept. 1768.

The following persons presented Petitions for Warrants of Survey on the Bounty having arrived on the Encouragement given by the late Act of the General Assembly.

	Acres	
Margaret Skillen	200	
John Skillen	100	In Berkley or Craven County.
Elizabeth Skillen	100	

ORDERED that the Secretary do prepare Warrants of Survey accordingly.

COUNCIL JOURNAL 34, page 250.
Meeting of Sept. 23, 1768.

Read the petition of George Wilks setting forth that he arrived in this Province from England about four months ago in the ship Little Carpenter Richard Maitland Commander on the encouragement of the Bounty given by this province and is now Engaged with Mr. De St. Pierre to go to Hillsborough Township to keep a School

ORDERED that the Secretary do prepare a Warrant of Survey & the public Treasurer to pay him the said Bounty

Council Journal 34, page 250.
Meeting of 30th. Sept. 1768.

His Honor informed the Board that some passengers had arrived lately from England who had come over to this Country with Expectations to receive the Bounty given by the Act of the General Assembly which Expired with the last Prorogation of the Assembly and therefore he desired there opinion if any on what Bounty poor protestants arriving in this Province under any Act of Assembly now in force. The Board advised his Honor to refer the matter to Mr. Attorney General to report his opinion thereon which his Honor was pleased to order accordingly.

Read the petition of John Rishton setting forth that he was a protestant and had arrived in this province twelve months ago on the encouragement of the Bounty and therefore humbly prayed to be allowed the same and also one hundred acres of land free of charge.

ORDERED that the prayer of his petition be granted and that the public Treasurer do pay him the said Bounty and that the Secretary do prepare a Warrant of Survey for 100 acres at or near the Long Canes or on Savannah River as prayed for by the Petitioner.

Council Journal 34, pages 252-255

IN THE COUNCIL CHAMBER
Tuesday the 4th. day of October 1768.
Present

His Honor the Lieut. Governor.
Othniel Beale
Egerton Leigh
Thomas Skottowe

His Honor the Lieutenant Governor informed the Board that Mr. Attorney General had waited on him with the following report on the matter referred to him on last Friday.

By the 6th. and 7th. paragraphs of the general duty Act passed the 14th. June 1751 three fifths of the Fund thereby raised within five years are to be paid to such poor protestants as come from Europe in that time and settle in the Southern and central parts of this province and after five years to such protestants settling any part of the province. The above Clauses by an Act of Assembly pass'd 7th. October 1752 are altered and amended by Extending the Bounty to such poor protestants settling in any part of the province for the time thereby limited and after the expiration of such time by appropriating for and during the continuance of the remainding term of the said Act the said fund by paying such poor protestants half Bounty only or in other words half the several sums pr. head as are allowed by this Act to such poor protestants as then were or should arrive here within the term of four months after passing the 1st Act by another Act passed the 25th. July 1761 the Legislature were pleased to increase the Bounty to such settlers and for that purpose appropriated Fund as therein is mentioned and repeal the Act of 7th. Oct'r 1752 and also enact that the 6th. and 7th. paragraphs of the general duty Act as far as the same relate to the applying the said three fifths of the Tax thereby imposed on negroes and other slaves and every matter and thing therein contained be from and after passing this Act absolutely repealed and vacated to all intents and purposes whatsoever by a reviving Act passed 23'd Jan'y 1765 and above of 25th. July 1761 for the repealing the aforesaid Clauses of the General Duty Act is revived and continued for three years and to the end of the then next General Assembly by another reviving Act passed 18th. April 1767 the General duty Act is revived and continued for five years and to the end of the then next Sessions of the General Assembly excepting the 6th. and 7th. Clauses thereof which appropriate the Tax thereby imposed the appropriation whereof by the Act passed 25th. July 1761 is otherwise directed and also excepting certain parts of the 35th. Clause of the said General duty Act which relates to other matters and likewise excepting such parts of the General duty Act as is hereby or by any other Act repealed by the prorogation which took place some time ago the Act of 1761 is now expired. Some passengers having lately arrived from England in expectation of receiving the Bounty given by the last mentioned Act; the Governor and Council therefore refer the matter to the Attorney General to report his opinion what claim of Bounty these people have upon the public under any of the above recited Acts. Pursuant to your Honors Order of the 30th. September last by advice of the Council I have stated such of the Bounty Acts as have at different times been passed by the Legislature of this province for the benefit of poor protestants and from a view of them it appears to me that the Act of 1761 which revived the General Duty Act Except the 6th. and 7th. Clauses thereof vested the Bounty affairs under the Act of 1761 which as it repealed the aforesaid Clauses and was then the only Act which directed the appropriation of the original Fund and this Act Terminating with the prorogation the Bounty was also ceased and therefore none can be legally given to the persons now applying for it Tho' I am of the opinion they are intitled under the Eighth Clause of the General Duty Act to their land free of charge.

EGERTON LEIGH
4th. October 1768.

And several of the people attending were called in and informed that the Act being expired they were intitled to no Bounty but when they were free they would be intitled to have their land free of charge.

Council Journal 36, Part 2, page 222-223.
Meeting of 8th. November 1772.

The following petitions praying to have Warrants of Survey were presented and Read.

	Acres		Acres
Hugh Ross	400	Elizabeth Thompson	100
John Walker	250	Mary Smith	100
John Caldwell	350	James Lavender	250
James Maffett	250	Robert Lavender	100
William McCleland	400	John Caldwell, Jun'r	100
John Boyd	150	George McCullough	100
James Leman	300	John Steel	100
Adam McCoy	100	John Caldwell	300
William Craig	300	James Mayer	300
John Wyly	100	James McGalliart	150
Andrew McCawly	150	James McGalliart	100
John McCully	100	Archibald Millar	100
Ephraim McCully	100	John Millar	100
Hugh Smith	450	William Millar, Sen'r	150

	Acres		Acres
William Millar, Jun'r	100	Samuel Leman	100
William Millar	250	James Nealy	250
George Neily	150	James Tufts	100
Agnes Neily	100	John Casky	200
Thomas Cameron	450	Daniel Dreand	100
Andrew Cooks	300	John McLelland	200
James Johnston	350	Rose McCleland	100
William McCluny	100	John McCleland, Jun'r	100
William McCleland, Jun'r	100	John Wenn	200
William McCleland	100	James Cample	200
David Atchison	200	Robert Campble	100
Hugh Abercrombie	200	Mary Campble	100
Samuel Neily	350	Hugh Campble	100
James Neily	100	John Martin	150
Mary Neily	100	James Daragh	350
Ann Russell	100	John Craig	100
Elizabeth Boyd	100	Rowley McCurley	250
John Boyd, Junior	100	Anthony Miller	300
David Boyd	100	Andrew Simpson	350
Robert Templeton	250	James Brown	100
James Templeton	100	William Templeton	150
Martha Templeton	100	In South Carolina,	
Agnes Templeton	100	on the Bounty.	
Robert Buchannan	100		

ORDERED that the Secretary do prepare Warrants of Survey as prayed for by the petitioners.

Council Journal 36, page 242-243.
Meeting of 1st December 1772.

The following Persons presented Petitions setting forth that they were Protestants and had lately come to settle in this Province with their Respective Familys from Ireland and were desirous to settle and cultivate some vacant lands in the back parts of this Country. But by Reason of their extreem Poverty they were altogether unable to pay the Fees due to the several offices for their Grants and that they were in hopes to have received some aid from the Province, as their Countrymen had hitherto done and therefore Prayed his Excellency to Grant them such Relief as in his Goodness he should see fit.

His Excellency thereupon observed to them that the Bounty given by the Province had ceased long since, & that they had no Reason from Government to expect any such assistance as they craved But it appearing that they were very poor his Excellency proposed to the several officers to deliver out their Warrants without expence to them and to take the Risk of being paid by the Public which they severally agreed to and the Secretary was Ordered to prepare Warrants of Survey for the undermentioned persons VIZ'T

	Acres		Acres
John Gamble	100	James Buchannon	100
Alexander Moore	200	Jane Buchannon	100
Margaret Moore	100	John Simpson	350
Agnes Moore	100	Jane Simpson	100
William Love	100	William Simpson	100
Mathew Love	100	Robert Simpson	100
Andrew McCausland	400	Andrew Wardnock	350
Mary McSwine	100	John Wardnock	100
John Henry	300	James McDonald	100
Agnes Young	100	George McDonald	450
Henry Young	100	John Holmes	300
Matthew Young	100	Jane Holmes	100
Samuel Anderson	100	James Holmes	100
George Buchannon	300	Andrew Holmes	100
Jane Buchannon	100	Mathew Holmes	100
John Buchannon	100	Rebecca Holmes	100
Henry Buchannon	100	Francis Holmes	100
William Buchannon	350	In South Carolina.	

Council Journal 36, page 242-245.
Meeting of 1st. December 1772.

Petitions from the undermentioned persons verified by their affidavits, setting forth that they were severally Protestants, and had arrived in this Province from Germany on the encouragement but that they never had received any Warrants for Lands & therefore Humbly Prayed for Warrants of Survey free of charge were presented and read VIZ'T

	Acres		Acres
Mary Shelly	100	Mary Riddlehober	100
Jacob Likey	100	Catherine Williams	100
John Isley	100	Margaret Black	100
Jacob Cooke	100	Michael Montz	100
Marg't Eliz'th Vittle	100	George Montz	100
Shalotha Bille	100	John Hipp	100
Ursula Mantz	100	Mary Tomanick	100
Ursula Myer	100	David Preesly	100
Catherine Sheely	100	William Douriss	100
Mary Vidle	100	Mary Eliz'th Kise	100
Ann Cooke	100	Mary Beckman	100
Margaret Seigler	100	Mary White	100
Christ'r Barbara Shoemaker	100	George Forster	100
Peter Williams	100	Dorothea Einsteller	100
Andrew Mires	100	Anna Magdelina Knights	200

ORDERED that the Secretary do prepared Warrants of Survey as prayed for by the Petitioners.

COUNCIL JOURNAL 37, page 15-25
Meeting of January 6, 1773.

The following persons who had lately arrived from Ireland into this province in the ship Lord Dunluce presented petitions for warrants of survey agreeable to their Respective Family Rights vizt

In South Carolina	Acres		Acres
Rev'd William Martyn	400	Hugh Owen	100
James H. Lurkam	300	John Owen	100
Robert Jamieson	250	Samuel Fear	250
Andrew Agnew	300	John Fleming	150
David Montgomery	350	John Craig	350
James Brown	350	John Greg	150
John Hewie	150	John Camble	300
John Rork	100	Robert Wilson	250
William Stormant	150	Gilbert McNary	250
John McChants	100	Jane Greg	100
Francis Adams	350	George Cherry	100
Mary Adams	100	John Mortant	100

	Acres		Acres
Hugh Douglass	100	Martha McQuillon	100
John Fleming	300	Janet McWilliam	100
Arch'd McWilliam	250	Agnes Allen	100
James Blair	250	James Crawford	200
Henry Rea	250	William Crawford	200
James Tweed	100	Alex'r Fleming	400
Adam McRory	150	William Miller	200
John Erving	150	Thomas Miller	100
John McLenan	300	William Miller	100
William McMurty	100	Robert Hannah	100
Mary Lidey	100	Robert Hannah	100
Will'm Moore	100	Charles Butnett	200
Thomas McClurken	100	Abraham Thomson	300
James McLurkam	100	Wm. Thomson	100
Samuel McLurkam	100	Mary Thomson	100
Mary McLurkam	100	Patrick McMichael	150
Eleanor McLurkam	100	Grizell Maybean	200
Lillas McLurkam	100	Henry Maybean	100
Jane McLurkam	100	John Maybean	100
Thomas Wilson	300	Thomas Maybean	100
Hugh Montgomery	100	Elizabeth Maybean	100
Robert Read	150	Samuel Irvine	150
Janet Smith	100	Christopher Strong	300
William Dial	100	Price Blair	100
Margaret Dial	100	Elizabeth McChants	100
John McCulloch	100	Robert Hove	250
Sarah Crellman	100	David Morrow	450
Charles Miller	200	Elizabeth Morrow	100
William Humphrey	100	Samuel Barber	200
David McQuestion	400	James Barber	100
James McQuestion	400	Isabel Barber	100
William Fairy	200	Joseph Barber	200
Thomas Creighton	100	John Beard	300
Thomas Creighton, jun'r	100	John Adams	100
Thomas Boggs	100	Rachael Adams	100
Samuel Miller	100	Agnes McKenley	100
Robert Walker	100	Wm. Adams	150
John McQuillon	200	William Miller	150
Mary McQuillon	100	Eliz'th Johnston	100

	Acres		Acres
James McClure	100	Robert Toad	100
John Wilson	100	Marg't Toad	100
John Hindman	100	Andrew Erving	100
Robert Bradford	350	John Erving	100
John Scott	300	Jannet Erving	100
William Scott	100	Elizabeth Erving	100
James Sloan	250	Jean Erving	100
John Lynn	200	Andrew Young	250
William Barlow	100	James Varner	300
Sarah Rea	100	Wm. Young	100
Francis Rea	200	Isabel Young	100
George McMaster	150	Janet Young	100
Patrick McMaster	100	Mary Young	100
John McMaster	100	Robert Karnahan	250
Hugh McMaster	100	Gilbert Reed	400
Martha McMaster	100	Hugh Reed	100
Ninian Greg	250	Margaret Beard	100
Archibald McKewn	250	Edmund Hooll	450
John McKewn	100	Charles Bryams	100
Mary McKewn	100	John McNary	100
George Daragh	200	Alex'r McNary	100
Robert Cowan	350	Andrew Wilson	100
James Craig	100	Dan'l Wilson	100
Mary Craig	100	Agnes Wilson	100
John Craig	100	William Teat	100
Mary Greg	100	James Spear	100
Richard Wright	150	Lillias Chambers	100
William Greg	150	Elizabeth Sheild	100
Thomas Weir	150	John McCalaster	100
David Weir	100	John Johnston	100
Thos. Weir	100	Margaret Craig	100
John Weir	100	John Cork	150
Archibald McNeil	250	Will'm McMaster	100
James Smith	150	Rachael Adams	100
Mary Stuart	100	Agnes Hannah	100
John Gelaspy	100	Mathew Fleming	100
Alexander McMullen	100	Sarah Kidd	100
James Tweed	100	Eliz'th Fleming	100
Eleanor Tweed	100	John McMurray	200

	Acres		Acres
John Semple	250	John McCalaster	100
Rowland Minlin	100	James Wilson	200

ORDERED that the Secretary do prepare Warrants of Survey as prayed for by the several Petitioners.

A List of passengers on board the Hopewell arrived in South Carolina and this day petitioned for Land VIZ't

	Acres		Acres
Alexander McKee	300	Ann M'Cree	100
Joseph Green	250	Sarah M'Cree	100
John Paterson	250	Susannah M'Cree	100
Robert M'Cree	250	Alexander M'Cree	100
Samuel Dunlap	250	James Gracy	250
William Gibson	350	John Gracy	100
James Gibson	100	Robert Gracy	100
James Gibson	150	Mary Gracy	100
Nicholas Gibbons	250	Martha Gibeney	100
John Kirkpatrick	350	William Miller	200

NB Those above the line able to pay for their warrants.

The undermentioned persons are not able to pay for their warrants.

	Acres		Acres
		Robert Hamilton	250
		Hugh Thomson	350
		William Dunlap	200
		Robert Dunlap	150
		Daniel M'Mullen	100
		James Young	100
James McKee	100	John Clarke	100
Charles McLelland	150	William Boyd	250
John Paterson	100	Joseph Menelly	250
William Paterson	350	Robert Gibson	100
Agnes Paterson	350	Margaret Gibson	100
William Bryson	350	John Shaw	100
Thomas Gray	150	George Gibson	400
Archibald Gray	250	John Smith	450
Samuel McCance	100	George Smith	100
John McCance	100	Alex'r Douglas	300
George Win	100	George Thomson	100
Robert Smith	350	John Beard	250
Samuel Clark	450	Mary Shepherd	100
James McBride	300	William Shanks	400

	Acres		Acres
Joseph Gracey	250	Alex'r Craig	100
Robert Mathews	300	John Stevenson	150
Elizabeth Mathews	100		
Margaret Mathews	100	ORDERED that the Secretary
Janet Paterson	100	do prepare Warrants of Sur-
James M'Cauley	100	vey as prayed for by the sev-
Robert Alexander	150	eral petitions.

A List of passengers arrived from Ireland in the ship Pennsylvania Farmer and this day petitioned for lands, viz.

	Acres		Acres
John Logue	400	James Harberson	150
James Moore	300	William Brown	400
James Phillips	250	Molly McRory	150
John Smith, Sen'r	250	Robert Callwell	450
Andrew Paterson	250	Thomas Scott	300
David M'Creight	150	Samuel Hall	150
William M'Creight	400	Andrew Spence	300
David M'Creight	200	Robert Spear	350
William Young	300	Henry Hearton	200
William Willey	350	James McMaster	250
Thomas Spence	350	James McConoughy	100
Archibald Todd	250	John Sproll	100
David Grimbs	400	David Miller	300
Nathaniel McDill	300	James Mann	200
John Cochran	100	James Barber	250
Samuel M'Cee	100	Mathew Mebin	150
John Smith, Jun'r	100	William Mebin	200
James Fairey	100	John M'Crory	100
David Dunn	100	Alexander Gaston	100
William McKeen	100	John Stinson	100
James McCreight	100	Agnes Walker	100
Ann Young	100	John McMurray	100
Francis Arthburthenet	450	James Hill	100
The above are able to pay.		Alexander McCauley	100
The undermentioned are not		Elizabeth Steen	100
able to pay.		Mary Leech	100
Hugh Waxon	350	Samuel Logue	100
Samuel Gamble	300	Agnes Waxen	100

	Acres		Acres
Eliz'th Waxon	100	Andrew Grumbs	100
Agnes Herbeson	100	Jean Grimbs	100
Mary Gaston	100	Mathew Grimbs	100
Jean Young	100	William Caldwell	100
Marrian M'Collough	100	Robert Caldwell	100
Mary Stinson	100	Anne Caldwell	100
William Scott	100	Agnes Elliott	100
John Miller	100	Francis Arthbuthnet	450
Eliz'th Miller	100	Jean Mouncy	100
James Spence	100	Robert Spence	100
Mary Spence	100	Jean Spence	100
Jean Spence	100	James Blair	350
Jean Todd	100	William Winbeck	100
Martha Meabin	100	John Longneck	100
Mary Meabin	100		
John Blear	100	ORDERED that the Secretary
John Brown	100	do prepare Warrants of Sur-
William Brown	100	vey as prayed for by the sev-
John Barber	100	eral petitions.

A list of the passengers who arrived in this Province from Ireland in the Brigantine Free Mason, & this day petitioned for land, viz.

	Acres		Acres
John Richey	100	Robert Thomson	100
John McKnight	350	John Thomson	100
Thomas McLeland	100	Isaac Livingston	300
Samuel Paterson	350	John Mullen	100
Robert Nisbett	400	John Brown	300
John Pressley	300	Edward McGreary	100
Samuel McKay	450	John Riddle	300

In South Carolina. Able to pay.

The undermentioned persons are not able to pay for their Warrants.

Henry Thomson	200	Jean Beard	100
William Thomson	100	Hugh Anderson	100
		Isabella Foster	100
		James Foster	100
		William Foster	300
		Sarah Foster	100
		Arthur McMachor	100
		Charles Coapling	150

	Acres		Acres
Alexand Coapling	100	Mary Patterson	100
William Coapling, Jun'r	100	John Thursdale	250
Jane Coapling	100	James Wilson	100
Margaret Bigham	150	Andrew Taylor	200
William Coapling	350	Mary Presley	100
Mary McKnight	100	James Breden	300
Jane McKnight	100	Chas. Stuart	100
Margaret McKnight	100	John Fleman	100
Hugh Gorley	100	William Shane	100
James Cox	300	Charles Coapling	100
William McKee	250	Cath'n Stevenson	100
Jonathan Nisbett	100	Rich'd McClurkam	150
Emila Eger	100	Wm. Reynolds	450
John Hall	250	Margaret Daniels	100
George Barnes	100	ORDERED that the Secretary	
Margaret Beard	100	do prepare Warrants as prayed	
William Beard	100	for by the several petitions.	

A List of Passengers who arrived in this province in the ship
————————— under the direction of Lewis De St. Pierre
and this day petitioned for land, viz.

	Acres		Acres
Theodore Brewer	200	Henry Jager	100
Mathias Cor	200	William Hook	100
John Bennet Slatter	100	Stephen Jeachin	100
Geor Lad Metzger	250	John Miolett	100
Arnuldus Rougimont	200	John Gottier	100
Nicholas Lafille	100	George Towbert	200
Will Saller	200	Samuel Steinich	100
Peter Gaillard	100	Jean Jacques Masle	100
Henry Abraham Shulles	200	John Sneider	100
John Willingham	100	Rosina Enharding	100
Jacob Pfeiffer	300	Barbara Enharding	100
Johan Barchinger	100		
William Pfaff	300	In South Carolina.	
Martif Ruppel	250	ORDERED that the Secretary	
Cloude Gaillard	100	do prepare Warrants as prayed	
Lowz Loraw Larrage	100	for by the several petitioners.	

COUNCIL JOURNAL 37, pages 37-38.

Meeting of 23 Jan. 1773.

A List of Passengers arrived in this Province from Ireland in the ship Britania, who this day petitioned for land, Viz't.

	Acres			Acres
Henry Graham	250	*These are able to pay for their Warr'ts.*	Sarah Carruthers	100
James Hutchison	100		John Kerr	200
William Dunlap	200		Jane Cochran	100
Peter Taaf	100		Hugh Cochran	100
Andrew Clarke	200		Martha Cochran	100
Samuel Russell	100		Agnes Cochran	100
James Getty	100		Margaret Cochran	100
Robert Craig	250		Robert Mathews	100
Mary Craig	100		James Bigham	250
James Craig	100		John Bigham	100
Anne Craig	100		Jane Bigham	100
Quintan Craig	100		James Hoey	200
Quintan McCreight	450	*These are poor people who have sworn they are not worth five pounds sterling.*	Alexander Clark	100
Agnes Rae	100		William Clark	100
Margaret McCullough	100		Jane Clark	100
John Campbell	350		Henry McInully	100
James Hamil	100		David Paterson	100
John Dunlap	250		John Mahagy	100
Margaret Dunlap	100		Henry Graham	250
Robert Dunlap	100		Mary Dunlap	100
William Dunlap, Jun'r	100		Thomas Martin	100
Alex'r Dunlap	100		Samuel Martin	250
David Thomson	200		William Beard	350
			Mary Telford	100
			James Beard	100

ORDERED that the Secretary do prepare Warrants of Survey as prayed for by the petitioners.

Index

A

Abercrombie, Hugh, 119.
Adair, Alex'dr, 74.
Adair, Alice, 71.
Adair, Andrew, 71.
Adair, James, 13, 74.
Adair, Jane, 9.
Adair, Margaret, 74.
Adair, Mary, 74.
Adams, Elizabeth, 12 (2).
Adams, Francis, 121.
Adams, John, 122.
Adams, Mary, 12, 121.
Adams, Rachel, 122, 123.
Adams, Sarah, 12.
Adams, Williams, 10, 122.
Adamson, George & wife, 46.
Admitz, Ber, 53.
Adolph, Henrick, 34, 37.
Adolph, Maria, 37.
Adolphin, Elizabeth, 39.
Adolphin, Catherine, 39.
Adory, Ann, 106.
Adory, Elizabeth, 106.
Adory, Martha, 106.
Adory, Thomas, 106.
Agey, Jane, 107, 109.
Agnew, Andrew, 121.
Agnew, Roger, 46.
Airs, Catherine, 84.
Airs, John, 82 (2).
Airs, Margaret, 82.
Airs, Susannah, 82.
Airs, Thomas, 82.
Airs, William, 82.
Albright, Anna, 38.
Albright, Eva, 38.
Albright, Mathew, 40.
Albrickten, Eva Elizabeth, 36.
Albrighten, Eva Elizabeth, 41.
Alexander, Alexander, 113.
Alexander, Elizabeth, 80.
Alexander, George, 80, 81.
Alexander, Robert, 81, 125.
Alexander, Samuel, 81.
Allardice, John, 113, 114.
Allen, Agnes, 122.
Allen, Violet, 71.
Almond, Catherine, 13.
Almond, James, 13.
Almond, John, 11, 13.
Alston, Samuel, 90.
Alston, William, 98.
Alvander, Johannes, 54.
Amelia Township, 43, 46.
Amnien, Martha, 22.

Amsterdam, 62.
Anclerson, Andrew, 57.
Ancrum, William, 64.
Anderson, Alexander, 69.
Anderson, Elizabeth, 70, 88.
Anderson, Hugh, 126.
Anderson, Johanes, 38.
Anderson, John, 67, 69, 88, 91.
Anderson, Mary, 69.
Anderson, Samuel, 120.
Anderson, William, 38, 67, 70.
Andrew, Alice, 89.
Andrew, Jane, 89.
Andrew, John, 13, 89 (2).
Andrew, Margaret, 89.
Andrew, Samuel, 89.
Andrew, William, 89.
Andrews, David, 78.
Andrews, Elizabeth, 78.
Andrews, John, 92.
Andrews, Mary, 78.
Andrews, William, 75, 78.
Angus, Hercules, 85.
Ansman, Anna Eva, 35.
Ausman, Catherine, 40.
Ausman, George, 40.
Anthony, Jean, 22.
Anweider, Anna Maria, 54.
Arbuche, John, 86.
Archer, Alexander, 107, 109.
Archer, Ann, 109.
Archer, Jane, 109.
Archer, Susannah, 109.
Archer, William, 109.
Archier, Ann, 73.
Archier, Isobella, 73 (2).
Archier, Mary, 73.
Archier, Robert, 71.
Archier, Rose, 73.
Archier, William, 71.
Ard, Jane, 77.
Ard, John, 74, 77 (2).
Ard, Mary, 77.
Armstrong, Margaret, 88, 91.
Armstrong, Mary, 88.
Armstrong, Samuel, 88, 91.
Armstrong, William, 88.
Arnet, Jannet, 71.
Arnot, Agnes, 74.
Arnot, George, 72.
Arnot, Jane, 72.
Arnot, Martha, 74.
Arnot, Samuel, 68.
Arthbuthnet, Francis, 126.
Arthburthenet, Francis, 125.
Arthur, George, 106.

Behler, Johan Jacob, 63.
Behler, Philip Jacob, 61.
Beidinger, John Jacob, 60.
Beldman, Samuel, 33.
Belfast Township, 5, 11, 14, 26, 28,
  32, 33, 43, 45, 47, 49, 58, 72.
Belfast (in Ireland), 46, 93.
Bell, Alexander, 97.
Bell, Eleanor, 79.
Bell, Elizabeth, 76, 80, 88, 91, 95, 96.
Bell, Isabell, 95.
Bell, James, 87, 91.
Bell, James, Jun'r, 87.
Bell, Jane, 97, 106.
Bell, John, 87, 94, 95 (2), 96, 97 (2),
  99.
Bell, Martha, 97, 99.
Bell, Mary, 7, 87, 88, 95.
Bell, Mathew, 75, 79.
Bell, Patrick, 68.
Bell, Robert, 104, 106.
Bell, Samuel, 87.
Bell, Sarah, 94 (2), 96 (2).
Bell, Thomas, 104, 106 (2).
Bell, William, 95 (2), 96 (2), 106.
Bellier, Jean Pierre, 21.
Belot, Pierre Hile, 21.
Belott, Marie Magdale, 21.
Bellott, Jean, 21.
Bend, Thomas William, 81.
Bennett, Robert, 65.
Bennison, Fanny, 68.
Bennison, George, 69.
Bennison, John, 67.
Bennison, Sarah, 69.
Bennison, William, 67.
Beraud, Mathew, 21, 22.
Beraud, (see Conton)
Berd, Phillip, 22.
Bercott, Conrad, 38.
Berry, Ann, 108, 110.
Berry, James, 108, 110.
Berry, Jane, 110.
Berry, Richard, 108, 110.
Berry, Robert, 108 (2), 110 (2).
Bert, John, 41.
Beryhill, Andrew, 48.
Biggam, Hugh, 110.
Biggam, James, 108, 110.
Biggam, John, 76.
Biggam, Joseph, 110.
Biggam, Margaret, 108, 110.
Biggam, Mary, 108, 110.
Biggam, Robert, 108 (2), 110 (2).
Bigham, James, 8, 128.
Bigham, Jane, 8, 128.
Bigham, John, 128.
Bigham, Margaret, 8, 127.
Bill, Lesslie, 71.

Bill, Margaret, 71.
Bill, William, 73.
Billaw, Antoine, 21.
Bille, Sharlotha, 121.
Bishop, Anne, Sen'r, 42.
Bishop, Anne, Jun'r, 42.
Bishop, John, 42.
Bishop, Mary, 42.
Black, David, 75, 79.
Black, Elizabeth, 81.
Black, Ester, 79.
Black, John, 48.
Black, Margaret, 121.
Black, Maria, 81.
Black, Mary, 81.
Black, Sarah, 79.
Black, William, 79.
Blair, George, 57.
Blair, James, 90, 122, 126.
Blair, Jane, 90.
Blair, Margaret, 90.
Blair, Price, 122.
Blair, Thomas, 90, 92.
Blair, William, 57.
Blake, Alice, 51.
Blake, Anne, 50.
Blake, David, 57.
Blake, John, 50.
Blake, Mary, 51.
Blakely, Chambers, 87, 91.
Blakely, David, 87, 91.
Blakely, Elizabeth, 87 (2), 91.
Blakely, Mary, 87.
Blakely, Sarah, 87, 91.
Blakely, William, 87, 91.
Blakly (see Blakely).
Blankheed, James, 108 (see also
  Bankheed).
Blear, John, 126.
Blemenskin, Anna, 38.
Bless, Casper, 61.
Blomhurt, Martin, 34.
Blumenhart, Martin, 37.
Blumentskin, Maria, 38.
Blumerstock, Andrew, 40.
Blundell, Catherine, 58.
Boats:
  Falls, 9.
  Prince Henry, 11.
  Dragon, 35, 40.
  Union, 35.
  Planters Adventure, 40.
  Frankland, 52, 55.
  London, 59.
  Britania, 62, 83, 128.
  Belfast Packet, 64.
  Hillsborough, 68.
  Earl of Hillsborough, 69.

Chipperwick, Hans Yorick, 54.
Chipperwick, Helena, 54.
Chipperwick, Johan, 54.
Claiter, Andrew, 53.
Clame, John, 36.
Clark, Alexander, 128.
Clark, Elizabeth, 83.
Clark, Jane, 83, 128.
Clark, Mary, 83.
Clark, Samuel, 124.
Clark, Thomas, 65, 82.
Clark, William, 128.
Clarke, Andrew, 128.
Clarke, John, 124.
Clem, Eliz'h, 36.
Clem, John, 41.
Clements, Goody, 26.
Clemmick, William, 51.
Clennick, Mary, 52.
Clennending, John, 104.
Clenningding, John, 105.
Clinton, Anthony, 57.
Clowny, Samuel, 72.
Cluzzeau, Pierre, 22.
Coapling, Alexander, 127.
Coapling, Charles, 126, 127.
Coapling, Jane, 127.
Coapling, William, 127.
Coapling, William, Jun'r, 127.
Coastre, Hans Yorrick, 53.
Cobran, John, 8.
Cochran, Agnes, 128.
Cochran, Hugh, 128.
Cochran, Jane, 128.
Cochran, John, 125.
Cochran, Margaret, 128.
Cochran, Martha, 128.
Cockran, Benjamin, 97, 98.
Cockran, David, 65.
Colvill, Matuerin, 6.
Congarees (river), 50.
Conn, John, 74, 77.
Conn, Patrick, 71.
Connolly, Mary, 86.
Connolly, Thomas, 57.
Conor, Mary, 109.
Conor, William, 107, 109.
Conton, Jean Beraud des, 22.
Cooey, Jane, 83.
Cooey, Jannet, 82.
Cooey, John, 83.
Cooey, Joseph, 83.
Cooey, Samuel, 81.
Cooey, William, 81, 83.
Cook, Ann, 73.
Cook, Eleanor, 73.
Cook, John, 73.
Cooke, Ann, 121.
Cooke, Jacob, 121.

Cooks, Andrew, 119.
Cooks, James, 71.
Cooper, Barbara, 86.
Copeland, John, 79.
Copland, John, 75.
Copnal, Jeremiah, 53.
Cor, Mathias, 127.
Cork, John, 123.
Corrie, Alexander, 72.
Corrie, Jane, 74.
Corrie, Margaret, 74 (2).
Corrie, Nicholas, 72.
Corrie, Robert, 74.
Corrie, William, 72, 74.
Corrough, Robert, 10.
Corry, George, 101, 102.
Corry, James, 101.
Corry, Jane, 102.
Corry, John, 101.
Cosby, Hannah, 10.
Cotteral, Catherine, 86.
Couney, Margaret, 109.
Counney, Margaret, 107, 109.
Courant, Barbara, 54.
Courants, Peter, 54.
Courents, Frederick, 55.
Courents, Lucet, 55.
Cowan, Robert, 123.
Cox, Ann, 78.
Cox, James, 127.
Cox, John, 75, 78.
Craig, Alex'r, 125.
Craig, Anne, 128.
Craig, Elizabeth, 75, 78.
Craig, George, 75, 78.
Craig, James, 123, 128.
Craig, John, 119, 121, 123.
Craig, Margaret, 123.
Craig, Mary, 78, 123, 128.
Craig, Quintan, 128.
Craig, Robert, 128.
Craig, William, 118.
Craine, Timothy, 33.
Cran, Frances, 52.
Craven County, 92, 103.
Crawford, Elizabeth, 75, 78.
Crawford, James, 57, 90, 92, 122.
Crawford, John, 100, 102.
Crawford, Joseph, 57.
Crawford, Marg't, 57.
Crawford, Samuel, 75, 78.
Crawford, William, 122.
Craymer, Peter, 53.
Crayton, Isaac, 72.
Cree, Johannes, 54.
Creighton, Thomas, 122.
Creighton, Thomas, Jun'r, 122.
Crellman, Sarah, 122.
Cress, David, 28.

Dodds, Jane, 83.
Dodds, John, 83 (2).
Dodds, Margaret, 82, 83.
Dodds, Martha, 83.
Dodds, Samuel, 82, 83.
Dodds, William, 83.
Doharty (see Dougharty also).
Doharty, James, 81 (2).
Doharty, Michael, 81.
Don, Jean, 21.
Donaldson, Hugh, 96.
Donalson, Hugh, 94.
Donalson, Mary, 94.
Doran, Johans, 40.
Dorchester Parish, 28.
Dorman, James, 80.
Dorn, Christian, 54.
Dorn, George, 34.
Dorn, Hester, 54.
Dorn, Margaretta, 54 (2).
Dorsen, George, 37.
Dorst, Peter, 35, 36, 60.
Dorst's, Anna Maria, 36.
Dorren, Anna Elizabeth, 37.
Dougal, Margaret, 86.
Dougharty (see Doharty also)
Dougharty, Ann, 83.
Dougharty, Daniel, 83.
Dougharty, Edward, 83.
Dougharty, John, 83.
Douglas, Alexander, 124.
Douglass, Agnes, 101.
Douglass, Alexander, 101.
Douglass, Hugh, 122.
Douglass, Isabell, 101.
Douglass, James, 101 (3), 103.
Douglass, Mary, 101 (2), 103.
Douglass, Robert, 101.
Douglass, Rose, 101.
Douglass, William, 97, 98.
Dourfour, Francis, 53.
Douriss, William, 121.
Dowdell, George, 9.
Downes, William, 75.
Downs, Ann, 80.
Downs, Mary, 80 (2).
Downs, Robert, 80.
Downs, William, 80.
Drafter (see Dafter also).
Drafter, John, 98.
Drayer, Henry, 114 (see Dryer also).
Dreand, Daniel, 119.
Dregg, John Peter, 15.
Dryer, Hendrick, 112 (see Drayer also).
Due, Mr., 29, 31.
Due, Daniel, 21.

Duerin, Rachel, 37 (see Derins also).
Duff, Hugh, 10.
Duffield, Anthony, 47.
Dunbar, Charles, 104, 106.
Dunbar, Oliver, 108, 110.
Duncan, David, 86.
Duncan, John, 75, 78.
Dunlap, Alex'r, 128.
Dunlap, John, 128.
Dunlap, Margaret, 128.
Dunlap, Mary, 128.
Dunlap, Robert, 124, 128.
Dunlap, Samuel, 124.
Dunlap, William, 92, 93, 124, 128.
Dunlap, William, Jun'r, 128.
Dunlop, Patrick, 28.
Dunn, Agnes, 101, 103.
Dunn, David, 76, 125.
Dunn, James, 101, 103 (2).
Dunn, Jane, 101.
Dunn, Mary, 86.
Dunsheth, James, 101, 102.
Dunsheth, Mary, 101.
Dunsheth, William, 101.
Dunsman, David, 90, 92.
Dunsman, Margaret, 90.
Dunwoodie, Wm., 9.
Duplici, Francis, 58.
Dupuy, Jean, 22.
Durin, Margaretta, 37 (see Derin also).
Duval, John, 114.
Duvall, John, 112.

E

Ebinger, Gotleb, 60.
Edelmansin, Anna Cara, 36.
Edelmansin, Anna Caradissin, 41.
Eddy, Mary, 58.
Egar, Robert, 72.
Eger, Emila, 127.
Egger, James, 11, 13.
Einsteller, Dorothea, 121.
Elbright, Christopher, 38.
Elliott, Agnes, 126.
Ellis, Ann, 108, 110.
Ellis, Esther, 110.
Ellis, Isabell, 69.
Ellis, James, 67.
Ellis, Joheph, 110.
Ellis, Margaret, 108, 110.
Ellis, Mary, 110.
Ellis, Robert, 108, 110.
Ellis, Sarah, 110.
Ellis, William, 108, 110.
Elsminger, Catherine, 14.
Elsminger, Catherine, Jun'r, 14.

138

Elsminger, Christian, 14.
Elsminger, Christian, Jun'r, 14.
Elsminger, Margaretta, 14.
Elsminger, Peter, 14 (2).
Elweany, James, 97, 98.
Embrigen, Elizabeth, 53.
Emekin, Elizabeth, 62.
Emmick, Anna Margaret, 63.
Emmick, Conrad, 63.
Emmick, Eliz'h, 63.
Emmick, Eva, 63.
Englet, Andrew, 53.
English & Lloyd, 107.
English, Andrew, 104, 106.
English, Jane, 106.
Enharding, Barbara, 127.
Enharding, Rosine, 127.
Erlbeck, Frederick, 37.
E(r)lbeck, George Fred'k, 34.
Erlbeck, Magdalen, 34.
Erlbeck, Maria, 40.
Erlbeck, Sophia, 37.
Erret, John, 54.
Erstern, Anna Maria, 63.
Erving, Andrew, 123.
Erving, Elizabeth, 123.
Erving, John, 122, 123.
Erving, Jannet, 123.
Erving, Jean, 123.
Erwine, Anne, 8.
Esksteyn, Dorothea, 64.
Estyhen, Catherine Eliz'h, 64.
Estyhens, Laurence, 61.
Eva, Hanna, 59.
Evashcoosnan, Anna, 46.
Eyksteyt, Henrick, 60.
Eyhsteen, Mary Mad'n, 60.
Eytinger, Barbara, 27.

F

Fairchild, Mr., 34.
Fairey, James, 125.
Fairy, William, 122.
Falman, Constantine, 53.
Fan, Anna Marg't, 62.
Fardor, Baddy, 74.
Fardor, Thomas, 72.
Fargar, James, 93.
Fargar, Margaret, 93.
Fargar, Thomas, 93.
Farquer, George, 113 (2).
Farrasteau, Anthoine, 22.
Farris, Mary, 101.
Farris, William, 101, 103.
Faulkner, Ann, 58.
Faulkner, Catherine, 58.
Fear, Samuel, 121.
Fee, Hugh, 9, 12.

Fee, John, 12.
Fee, Margaret, 12 (2).
Fee, Mary, 12.
Fee, Rachel, 12.
Fee, Sarah, 9.
Fee, Susannah, 12.
Fegart, Michael, 65.
Fellows, Abram, 45.
Fellows, Anne, 45.
Fellows, Eliz'th, 45.
Fellows, Helen, 45 (2).
Fellows, Mary, 45.
Feltman, Anna Catherine, 40.
Feltman, Elizabeth, 37, 40.
Feltman, George, 35, 37.
Fenshaw, Daniel, 27.
Ferdinand, Catherine, 36.
Ferdinand, Johan Fred'k, 41.
Ferdinand, John Hen., 36.
Ferguson, Duncan, 87.
Files, Stephen, 42 (2).
Fillips, Elizabeth, 99.
Fillips, Jane, 99 (2).
Fillips, John, 99 (2), 102.
Fillips, Mary, 99.
Fillips, Robert, 99 (2), 102.
Finerman, Jared, 53.
Fink, Catherine, 54.
Fink, Hans Yorick, 54.
Fink, Margaretta, 54.
Finly, John, 96.
Fisher, Samuel, 47.
Fisherin, Anna Maria, 62.
Fitting, Nicholas, 43.
Fleman, John, 127.
Fleming, Alexander, 100, 102, 122.
Fleming, Eliz'th, 123.
Fleming, George, 72.
Fleming, Hannah, 105.
Fleming, James, 100, 102, 103, 105.
Fleming, John, 100, 121, 122.
Fleming, Mary, 100.
Fleming, Mathew, 123.
Fleming, Ralph, 71.
Fleming, Robert, 71.
Fleming, William, 103, 105.
Flick, Johannes, 35, 36.
Flick, John George, 114.
Flick, Johannes Gerlogh, 112.
Flick, Hans George, 60.
Flicken, Barbara, 36.
Flicken, Eva, 36.
Flicken, Henrietta, 36.
Flicken, Sabina, 36.
Flint, Elizabeth, 98.
Flint, Hannah, 98, 99.
Flint, John, 98.
Flugell, Melchor, 37.
Fonses, Postian, 28.

Greg (see Torrens).
Greg, John, 121.
Greg, Jane, 121.
Greg, Mary, 123.
Greg, Ninian, 123.
Greg, William, 123.
Gregg, Hugh, 72.
Gregg, John, 26.
Gregg, Joseph, 47.
Gregg, Thomas, 11.
Grelling, John, 113 (2).
Grey, Martilla, 54.
Greison, Catherine, Sen'r, 32.
Greison, Catherine, Jun'r, 32.
Grierson, George, 32.
Grierson, Jane, 32.
Griffen, Isobell, 80.
Griffen, Jane, 80.
Griffen, John, 76, 80.
Griffen, Rose, 80.
Griffen, William, 80.
Grimbs, David, 125.
Grimbs, Jean, 126.
Grimbs, Matthew, 126.
Groo, Teresia, 54.
Groo, Valentine, 54.
Gros, Francois, 22.
Gross, Frans, 13.
Grubert, Johan, 35, 41.
Grumbs, Andrew, 126.
Guess, Henrick, 62.
Guilhibaw, Andrew, 22.
Gurly, John, 45.
Gutt, Adam, 60.

H

Haag, Johannes, 38.
Hagen, Anna Maria, 41.
Hagen, Dorothea, 40.
Hagen, Margaret, 40.
Hagin, Ann Maria, 35.
Hainsworth, Enoch, 14.
Halifax, 111.
Halgerman, Peter, 53.
Hall, Alexander, 89, 91.
Hall, Charles, 89.
Hall, Clark, 89, 91.
Hall, George, 89 (2), 92.
Hall, James, 89.
Hall, Jane, 89.
Hall, John, 82, 90, 127.
Hall, Margaret, 84.
Hall, Mary, 89.
Hall, Robert, 50.
Hall, Samuel, 89, 125.
Hall, William, 89, 90, 91.
Ham, Henrick, 41.
Hambleton, James, 75.

Hamel, Christopher, 34.
Hamell, Christopher, 36.
Hamelin, Maria, 36.
Hamil, James,·128.
Hamilton, Agnes(s), 73, 79.
Hamilton, Alexander, 75, 79.
Hamilton, James, 78.
Hamilton, Jenny, 101.
Hamilton, John, 6, 88, 91.
Hamilton, Lilly, 73.
Hamilton, Mary, 101.
Hamilton, Nelly, 101.
Hamilton, Patrick, 101, 103.
Hamilton, Robert, 124.
Hamilton, Samuel, 71, 73.
Hammett, Captain, 35, 40.
Hannah, Agnes, 123.
Hannah, Alexander, 8.
Hannah, Andrew, 92, 93.
Hannah, Capt., 76, 80.
Hannah, Elias, 79.
Hannah, James, 75, 79, 108, 109.
Hannah, Mary, 79.
Hannah, Richard, 79.
Hannah, Robert, 75, 79, 122 (2).
Hannah, Sophia, 79.
Hannah, William, 47.
Hanon, Anna Eliz'h, 36.
Hanold, David, 41.
Hansilmanin, Eprosina, 61.
Hansilmanin, Mary Eliz'th, 64.
Hanvey, Jane, 70.
Hanvey, Sarah, 70.
Hanvey, William, 67.
Harbeson, Agnes, 126 (Herbeson).
Harbeson, James, 125.
Harbison, Adam, 89, 92.
Harbison, Elizabeth, 89.
Harbison, James, 89.
Harbison, Jane, 89.
Harbison, Jannet, 89.
Harbison, John, 89.
Harbison, Mary, 89 (2), 91.
Harbison, Patrick, 89, 91.
Harkins, Elizabeth, 74.
Harkins, Hugh, 72.
Harper, Agnes, 93.
Harper, Benjamin, 92, 93.
Harper, Daniel, 92, 93.
Harper, Donald, 49.
Harper, James, 92, 93.
Harper, Jane, 93.
Harper, John, 93 (2).
Harper, Margaret, 93.
Harper, Martha, 93.
Harper, Robert, 92, 93.
Harper, William, 92 (2), 93 (3).
Harrison, Arthur, 76, 80.
Harshaw, Daniel, 82.

Hart, Elizabeth, 73.
Hart, George, 73.
Hart, Jacob, 71.
Hart, Susannah, 73 (2).
Hartmutz, John Balker, 53.
Hartness, David, 78.
Hartness, Jane, 78.
Hartness, Jannet, 78.
Hartness, Nath'l, 75.
Hartness, Nathan, 78.
Hartwild, Johannes, 54.
Hartwild, John Jacob, 55.
Hartwild, Petrus, 55.
Harvey, Mary, 68.
Hasseroot, Christian, 56.
Hathorn, Adam, 94, 96.
Hathorn, Benjamin, 94.
Hathorn, Elizabeth, 94 (2).
Hathorn, James, 6 (2), 94, 96.
Hathorn, John, 94 (2), 96 (2).
Hathorn, Joseph, 94.
Hathorn, Mary, 94, 96.
Hathorn, Robert, 94.
Hauck, Catherine, 63.
Hauck, Elizabeth, 63.
Hauck, Johannes, 61.
Hauck, Magdalina, 63.
Hauffmanin, Eve Eliz'h, 64.
Hauffmanin, Leonard, 64.
Hawn, Ann Eliz'th, 36.
Hay, Jean Bell, 21.
Hay, Robert, 77.
Hay, William, 74, 77.
Hearse, John, 66.
Hearse, John, Jun'r, 66.
Heartly, Robert, 65.
Hearton, Henry, 125.
Heller, Francis, 114.
Heme, Adam, 35.
Hen, Barbara, 39.
Hen, Nicholas, 39.
Hen, John Fred'k, 39.
Hen, Margaret, 39.
Hendrick, Alexander, 86.
Henhogs, George, 33.
Henery, Agnes, 109.
Henery, Alexander, 109.
Henery, Elizabeth, 109 (2).
Henery, Hugh, 109.
Henery, John, 109 (2).
Henry, Agnes, 107.
Henry, Alexander, 107.
Henry, John, 107, 120.
Henning, Ann, 73.
Henning, Anne, 73.
Henning, Hannah, 73.
Henning, James, 71, 94, 96.
Henning, Jane, 71, 73.
Henning, Mary, 73.

Henning, Michael, 71.
Henning, Robert, 71, 73.
Herlebeck, John, 33.
Herman, Andrew, 71.
Herman, Christian, 73.
Hermersmith, Johan Jacob, 41.
Hern, Johannes, 62.
Herne, Peter, 35.
Hero, Francis, 60.
Heron, James, 68.
Heron, Jane, 8.
Heron, Robert, 8.
Heron, William, 8.
Herr, Eva Catherine, 63.
Herr, Jacob, 61.
Herring, Anna Elizabeth, 61.
Herring, George Zachary, 61.
Herring, John George, 61.
Herring, Maria Catherine, 61.
Herthrington, Edward, 68.
Hewie, John, 121.
Hewitt, James, 66.
Hewson, David, 86.
Heydel, Anna Teresia, 54.
Heydel, Catherine Ester, 54.
Heydel, Conrad Fred'k, 54.
Heydel(l), Hester, 54.
Heydel, Johan Jacob, 54.
Heydel(l), Werra, 54.
Heyder, Anna Helena, 54.
Heyder, Nicholas, 53.
Heyhen, Anna Maria, 60.
Heyland, Ann, 84.
Heyland, Peter, 82.
Heyler, Johan Jacob, 54.
Heyley, Angelica, 50.
Heysher, Peter, 19.
Heynard, Archibald, 112.
Hibler, Edward (see McHibler).
Higgins, Thomas, 15.
Higginson, Ann, 76, 80.
Hill, James, 125.
Hill, Margaret, 109.
Hill, Thomas, 107, 109.
Hill, Samuel, 107, 109.
Hill, Susannah, 107, 109.
Hill, William, 109.
Hillary, John, 94, 96.
Hillsborough (Englishman), 19.
Hillsborough Township, 59, 80, 112,
  114, 115.
Hindman, John, 123.
Hinton, Eleanor, 110.
Hinton, Hannah, 110.
Hinton, Robert, 108, 110.
Hipp, John, 121.
Hodge, Alexander, 94.
Hodge, Elizabeth, 94.
Hodge, Francis, 94, 96.

Jones, Mary, 73.
Jones, Nathan, 85.
Jones, Robert, 71, 72, 73.
Jones, Samuel, 73.
Jones, Thomas, 66.
Jones, William, 71, 73.
Joor, Christian, 63.
Joor, Margaretta, 62, 63.
Joor, Maria Elizabeth, 62.
Jordan, Ann, 74.
Jordan, Elizabeth, 78.
Jordan, Isobell, 75.
Jordan, Isobell, 78.
Jordan, Jane, 75, 78.
Jordan, Margaret, 78.
Jordan, Martha, 75, 77.
Jordan, Thomas, 75, 78.

K

Kain, John, 57.
Kaine, Susanna, 57.
Kanny, Agnes, 100.
Kanny, Alexander, 100, 102.
Kanny, Isabell, 100.
Kanny, Margaret, 100.
Karnahan, Robert, 123.
Kaufman, Aaron, 53.
Kays, Malcom, 72.
Keas, James, 108.
Keas, Jane, 110.
Keen, Valentine, 35.
Keibber, Peter, 41.
Keiss, Anna, 39.
Keiss, Ann Eliz'h, 34.
Keiss, Catherine, 37.
Keiss, Elizabeth, 37.
Keiss, Eva, 37 (2).
Keiss, Gothel, 40.
Keiss, Hans Adam, 39.
Keiss, Maria, 37, 39.
Keiss, Maria Cath'a, 35.
Keiss, Michael, 35.
Keiss, Nicholas, 37.
Keiss, Phil, 34.
Keiss, Philip, 37.
Keiterin, Barbara, 36.
Keleigh, Eva, 53.
Keleigh, John George, 53.
Keleigh, Maria Dorothea, 53.
Keller, Andreas, 62.
Keller, Anna Marg't, 64.
Keller, Daniel, 60.
Keller, Eva, 64.
Keller, John, 64.
Keller, John George, 64.
Keller, John Philip, 64.
Keller, Margaret, 64.
Keller, Margaretta, 64.

Keller, Maria, 64.
Keller, Theobold, 64.
Keller, Peter, 61.
Kellet, Francis, 112.
Kelly, Joseph, 71.
Kelly, Simon, 71.
Kelsey, Stephen, 54.
Kelso, Elizabeth, 88.
Kelso, George, 88, 91.
Kelso, Isabell, 88.
Kelso, Jannet, 88, 91.
Kelso, John, 88.
Kelso, Margaret, 88.
Kelso, Samuel, 88 (2), 91.
Kelso, Susan, 88.
Ken, Adam, 37.
Kendar, Anna Eva, 27.
Kenmerling, Mathew, 14 (see Kem-
    merling also).
Kenn, Anna Eliz'h, 37.
Kenn, Eliz'h, 37.
Kenn, Peter, 37.
Kennedy, Agnes, 13.
Kennedy, Alexander, 9, 11, 13.
Kennedy, David, 75, 79.
Kennedy, Eleanor, 107.
Kennedy, Elizabeth, 13, 79, 109.
Kennedy, James, 57, 79, 94, 96.
Kennedy, John, 13, 67, 79, 107, 109.
Kennedy, Margaret, 69, 79, 107, 109.
Kennedy, Robert, 13, 107, 109.
Kennedy, William, 13.
Kennern, George Michael, 35, 41.
Kenny, John, 82.
Kenny, William, 82.
Kensey, David, 81.
Kentarin, Barbara, 41.
Kentzen, Andreas, 36.
Kentzem, Catherine, 36.
Kerber, Hans Adam, 60.
Kerbs, Michael, 53.
Kerlesford (see Carlesford also).
Kerlesford, Anna Maria, 53.
Kerner, George, 53.
Kerr, James, 75, 76, 78.
Kerr, John, 128.
Kerrs, James, 7.
Keuterin, Eliz'h, 36.
Key, William, 71.
Keyester, Nicholas, 53.
Keynal, Johan, 53.
Keysher, Peter, 61, 63.
Khunn, Anna Maria, 37.
Khunn, Barbara, 37.
Khunn, George, 39.
Khunn, John Henry, 39.
Khunn, Peter, 41.
Khunn, Valentine, 37.
Kibler, Irig Adam, 60.

Laird, Mary, 70.
Laird, Samuel, 70.
Lamont, Alice, 90.
Lamont, James, 90, 92.
Lamont, John, 90.
Lande, Francis La, 112.
Lang, George Henry, 64.
Lang, Jacob, 60.
Lang, Johannes, 63.
Lang, Johannes Martin, 63.
Lang, Maria Christian, 60, 63, 64.
Lang, Maria Eliz'h, 63.
Lang, Thomas, 61.
Langell, Jacque, 21, 22.
Langell, Pierre, 22.
Langwalt, Johan, 41.
Larne, 99.
Larrage, Lowz Loraw, 127.
Latham, Richard, 108.
Latou, Anne, 22.
Latou, Susanna, 22.
Laurens, Henry, Esq., 86.
Lavender, James, 118.
Lavender, Robert, 118.
Lavery, John, 8.
Law, George, 12.
Law, Isiah, 13.
Law, Jane, 12, 13.
Law, John, 10.
Law, Robert, 12.
Law, William, 10, 12.
Lawfin, James, 75, 79.
Lawfin, Mary, 79.
Lawfin, Samuel, 75, 79.
Leard, Samuel, 67.
Lee, Nicholas, 72.
Leech, Mary, 125.
Lefay, Jean, 21.
Leg, William, 105.
Legg, William, 103.
Leigh, Egerton, 116, 118.
Leithgon, William, 71.
Leman, James, 118.
Leman, Michael, 34.
Leman, Samuel, 119.
Lemmon, Gilbert, 10.
Lender, Anna Maria, 64.
Lepol, Peter, 80.
Leoron, Mr., 29, 31.
Leoron, Piere, 21.
LeQue, Magdaline, 112.
LeRoy, Peter Mich'l, 114.
Lesslie, Ann, 48.
Leslie, James, 10.
Lesslie, Jane, 10, 12, 48 (3).
Lesslie, John, 9, 47, 48.
Lesslie, Mart., 48.
Lesslie, Mary, 48.
Lesslie, Samuel, 48.

Lesslie, Thomas, 47, 48.
Lesslie, William, 48 (2).
Lester, George, 103, 107.
Lethem, Andrew, 108, 109 (2).
Lethem, Jane, 109.
Lethem, Moses, 109.
Lethem, Richard, 109 (see Latham also).
Lathem, Robert, 109.
Lethem, Sarah, 109.
Lethgon, Elizabeth, 73.
Lethgon, Rother, 73.
Levinston, Jean, 9.
Levinston, John, 9.
Levinston, Margaret, 12 (2).
Levinston, Mary, 12.
Levinston, Robert, 12.
Levinston, William, 9.
LeViolette, Ensign, 29, 31.
Levis, Mary, 104.
Lewers, James, 76 (2), 80.
Lewers, Michael, 76, 80.
Lewis, James, 72, 80.
Lewis, Richard, 86.
Lidey, Mary, 122.
Likey, Jacob, 121.
Lindaner, George Henry, 13.
Linden, Henry, 67.
Linder, Arabella, 69.
Lindley, Elizabeth, 69.
Lindsay, Agnes, 70.
Lindsay, Elizabeth, 70 (2).
Lindsay, Isabella, 67.
Lindsay, James, 7, 70.
Lindsay, Jane, 72.
Lindsay, Margaret, 12.
Lindsay, Thomas, 70.
Lindsay, Samuel, 67, 68.
Lindsay, William, 9.
Lindsey, Agnes, 69.
Lindsey, Hannah, 97, 99.
Lindsey, John, 67, 69.
Lindsey, Robert, 69.
Lindsey, Sarah, 72.
Lindsey, Thomas, 67.
Lirister, Joseph, 53.
Lister, Jane, 82.
Little, Anne, 8.
Little, John, 26.
Little, William, 8, 67.
Livingston, Isaac, 126.
Livingston, Joseph, 75, 78.
Loan, James, 75.
Loan, Mary, 75.
Lockhart, Catherine, 79.
Lockhart, David, 75, 79.
Lockyer, Barbara, 56.
Lockyer, Jacob, 56.
Loggan, Mary, 94.

Loggan, John, 94.
Loggan, Thomas, 94, 96.
Loggan, William, 94.
Logue, John, 125.
Logue, Samuel, 125.
Lonley, Captain, 40.
London, 35, 38, 39, 40.
Londonborough Township, 40, 41, 43, 47, 56.
Londonderry, 97.
Long Canes, 5, 30, 50, 51, 59, 66, 80, 81, 82, 92, 116.
Long, John, 104, 106.
Longneck, John, 126.
Loury, James, 94.
Love, Mathew, 120.
Love, William, 120.
Lowe, Thomas, 86.
Lowey, John, 94.
Lowey, Robert, 94.
Lowrey, John, 72.
Lowry, James, 96.
Lowry, John, 57.
Lowry, Robert, 96.
Luke, Alexander, 108.
Luke, Andrew, 109.
Lurkam, James H., 121.
Lynn, John, 123.
Lyon, John, 51.
Lyttleton, Fort, 22, 24, 25.

M

Mach, Charles, 15.
Machor, Arthur, 126.
Macguire, Ann, 58.
Maffett, James, 118.
Magee, John, 71.
Magelton, Andrew, 94, 96.
Magelton, Elizabeth, 94, 96.
Magelton, James, 94, 96.
Magelton, Peter, 94.
Magelton, Vance, 94, 96.
Magilton, John, 71.
Magilton, William, 71.
Maginsay, Thomas, 72.
Mahaffy, Martha, 93.
Mahaffy, Martin, 93, 95.
Mahaffy, Mary, 93.
Mahagy, John, 128.
Maitland, Richard, 115.
Major, David, 70.
Major, Eliz'h, 70.
Major, Ester, 70.
Major, James, 67.
Major, John, 67.
Major, Mary, 70.
Major, William, 67.
Man, James, 90.

Man, Jannet, 90.
Man, John, 90.
Man, Robert, 90 (2), 92.
Man, Susannah, 90.
Mann, James, 125.
Mannary, John, 95, 96.
Manning, Richard, 57.
Manson, Jane, 86.
Mantz, Ursulla, 121.
Mantzor, Elizabeth, 54.
Mantzor, Henrick, 54.
Mark, Agnes, 78.
Mark, Rose, 78.
Mark, Samuel, 75, 78.
Mark, Sarah, 78.
Marks, Andrew, 35.
Marks, William, 51.
Marque, Henry, 114.
Marshall, Elizabeth, 90.
Marshall, Jane, 90, 92.
Marshall, Jannet, 90.
Marshall, Mary, 90.
Marshall, Robert, 90.
Marshall, William, 90, 92.
Marskin, Barbara, 37.
Martin, Andrew, 100.
Martin, David, 5.
Martin, Francis, 6.
Martin, James, 57, 100 (2), 102.
Martin, Jane, 100(2).
Martin, John, 6, 9, 100, 119.
Martin, Mary, 5, 76, 80.
Martin, Peter, 32, 33.
Martin, Robert, 57.
Martin, Samuel, 128.
Martin, Sarah, 6.
Martin, Thomas, 75, 80, 104, 106, 128.
Martin, William, 72, 75, 80, 100.
Martyn, Rev. William, 121.
Masle, Jean Jacques, 127.
Mather, Martha, 48.
Mathews, Elizabeth, 6, 125.
Matthews, George, 14.
Mathews, John, 113.
Mathews, Margaret, 125.
Mathews, Robert, 125, 128.
Mathew(s), Sophia, 14.
Maurer, Eliz'h, 63.
Maxwell, Alex'r, 48.
Maxwell, Jane, 48.
Maxwell, John, 47, 48.
Maxwell, Nicholas, 48.
Maxwell, Robert, 48.
Maybean, Elizabeth, 122.
Maybean, Grizell, 122.
Maybean, Henry, 122.
Maybean, John, 122.
Maybean, Thomas, 122.

148

Mayer, Eva Maria, 14.
Mayer, James, 118.
Mayer, Philip Jacob, 14.
Mayer, Godfreid, 14.
Meabin, Martha, 126.
Meabin, Mary, 126.
Mebin, Mathew, 125.
Mebin, William, 125.
Meglamery, Hannah, 106.
Meglamery, William, 104, 106.
Mehl, Anna Maria, 37.
Mehl, Moria, 39.
Mehl, Peter, 34, 37.
Mellett, Hanrick, 53.
Melz, Anna Margaretta, 64.
Melz, John Valentine, 64.
Melz, Maria Catherine, 64.
Menelly, Joseph, 124.
Menningon, Jacob, 53.
Merck, Henrick, 39.
Merk, Anna Maria, 39.
Merk, Balker, 35.
Merk, Belshazer, 37.
Merk, Conrad, 37. (See Muck).
Merk, Eliz'h, 37.
Merk, Jacob, 39.
Merk, Locenty, 37.
Merk, Rosina, 37.
Merk, Susannah, 37.
Merking, Catherine, 61.
Merks, Andrew, 37.
Merkson, Anna, 40.
Mert, Maria Eva, 55.
Mert, Yorick, 55.
Merts, Cunninghand, 54.
Merts, Michael, 54.
Merwitz, Johan, 53.
Merwitz, Kahlba, 53.
Merwitz, Murza, 53.
Messersmith, Eva Cath., 36.
Messersmith, Johan Jacob, 36.
Metland, John, 75, 78.
Metland, Marg'rt, 78.
Metz, Christopher, 60.
Metzer, Johan Mathew, 35, 41.
Metzger, Geor. Lad, 127.
Michael, John, 50.
Michael, Valentine, 41.
Michael, Barbara, 41.
Mike, Peter, 53.
Mickell, Johannes Adam, 62.
Miles, Elizabeth, 8.
Miles, Thomas, 8.
Millar, Archibald, 118.
Millar, John, 118.
Millar, William, 119.
Millar, William, Sen'r, 118.
Millar, William, Jun'r, 119.
Millen, John, 78.

Miller, Agnes, 84.
Miller, Anthony, 119.
Miller, Charles, 122.
Miller, David, 125.
Miller, Eliz'th, 126.
Miller, John, 82, 126.
Miller, Paul, 45.
Miller, Robert, 101, 102.
Miller, Samuel, 122.
Miller, Thomas, 122.
Miller, William, 122 (3), 124.
Milligan, John, 72.
Minges, Conrad, 61, 63.
Minlin, Rowland, 124.
Miot, Jane, 58.
Miolett, John, 127.
Mires, Andrew, 121.
Miscample, James, 68, 69.
Miscample, John, 68.
Miscample, Mary, 69.
Miscample, Robert, 69.
Miskilly, Edward, 71.
Miswillering, Maria, 36.
Mitchell, David, 86.
Moin(e), Robert, 76, 80.
Mole, Dorothy, 15.
Mole, John George, 15.
Monford, John, 108, 111.
Montgomery, Agness, 80.
Montgomery, David, 121.
Montgomery, Elizabeth, 75, 78.
Montgomery, George, 75, 78, 79.
Montgomery, Henry, 68.
Montgomery, Hugh, 6, 122.
Montgomery, James, 65, 78.
Montgomery, John, 10, 67, 75, 78.
Montgomery, Latitia, 69.
Montgomery, Mary, 75, 78.
Montgomery, Rachel, 69.
Montgomery, Robert, 104.
Montgomery, Samuel, 69.
Montgomery, William, 69.
Montz, George, 121.
Montz, Michael, 121.
Moor, Andrew, 93, 96.
Moor, Ann, 94.
Moor, Christopher, 94.
Moor, Elizabeth, 94, 96.
Moor, Elnor, 94.
Moor, Izrael, 94 (2), 96 (2).
Moor, Jane, 94, 96.
Moor, John, 13, 94.
Moor, Nancy, 94.
Moor, Richard, 94, 96.
Moor, Thomas, 13.
Moor, William, 13, 94, 96.
Moore, Agnes, 79, 87, 91, 120.
Moore, Alexander, 120.
Moore, Ann, 48, 105.

155

Reid, John, 77.
Reid, Mathew, 74, 77.
Reid, Mary, 69, 77 (2).
Reid, Robert, 67, 86.
Reid, Sarah, 69, 77.
Reid, William, 69.
Reily, William, 57.
Repscher, Anna Marg'ta, 63.
Repscher, Johan, 63.
Repscher, Maria Catherina, 63 (2).
Rets, Anthony, 61.
Retz, Catherine, 56.
Revere, Laurens, 112.
Revierre, Laurens, 114.
Rew, John Petty, 33.
Reyley, David, 27.
Reyley, James, 27.
Reyley, John, 27.
Reyley, Mary, 27.
Reyley, Samuel, 27.
Reymor, Michael, 53.
Reynolds, Andrew, 71.
Reynolds, Henry, 73.
Reynolds, James, 73.
Reynolds, Margaret, 73.
Reynolds, Robert, 76, 80.
Reynolds, William, 73, 127.
Rhoderin, John, 26.
Rice, George, 19.
Richardson, Samuel, 82.
Richey, John, 126.
Richman, Jacob, 53.
Rickert, Jacob, 14.
Riddle, John, 126.
Riddlehober, Mary, 121.
Riggen, Barbara, 60.
Rits, Christian, 63.
Rits, Sophia, 63.
Roache, Michael, 76.
Robert, Alexander, 125.
Robertson, John, 82.
Robertson, William, 82.
Robins, Isabell, 106.
Robins, Jane, 106.
Robins, John, 104, 106.
Robinson, Alexandar, 68.
Robinson, George, 76.
Robinson, Grizil, 76.
Robinson, James, 74, 76.
Robinson, Jane, 84, 89, 91.
Robinson, John, 76, 89, 91, 108, 110.
Robinson, Margaret, 84, 89.
Robinson, Mary, 91.
Robinson, Robert, 89 (2), 91.
Robinson, Robert, Jun'r, 91.
Robinson, Sarah, 84.
Robinson, Susannah, 89.
Robinson, Thomas, 76, 89, 91.
Robinson, Waterhouse, 89.

Robinson, William, 68.
Rodgers, Agnes, 93.
Rodgers, Catherine, 78.
Rodgers, Elizabeth, 78.
Rodgers, Jannet, 75, 78.
Rodgers, Robert, 75.
Rodgers, William, 92, 93.
Rodman, Francis, 78.
Rodeman, Francis, 75.
Roe, Elizabeth, 74.
Roe, John, 72.
Roe, Susannah, 74.
Roger, Mr., 29, 30, 31.
Roger, Jean, 21.
Roger, Piere, 21.
Rogers, Downy, 80.
Rogers, Elizabeth, 79.
Rogers, Jane, 79.
Rogers, John, 79.
Rogers, Margaret, 79.
Rogers, Marie, 21.
Rogers, Mary, 79.
Rogers, Robert, 79, 112, 114.
Rogor, Jeremiah, 21.
Rolland, Piere, 22.
Ropsher, John Wellen, 61.
Roquemore, Pierre, Jeun, 22.
Roquemore, Pierre, Anne, 22.
Roquemore, Susanna, 22.
Rork, John, 121.
Ross, Andrew, 65.
Ross, Hugh, 118.
Ross, Jane, 67.
Ross, Martha, 69.
Ross, Thomas, 67.
Ross, William, 67.
Rothmeyer, Erhert, 61.
Rothmeyer, Eva Maria, 61.
Rothmeyer, George, 61.
Rotterdam, 55.
Rougimont, Arnuldus, 127.
Rounds, George, 28.
Rousen, Maria Elizabeth, 36.
Rouson, Andreas, 41.
Rouson, Andrew, 36.
Rouson, Anna Maria, 36.
Rouson, Maria Elizabeth, 41.
Rouson, Rudolph, 36.
Rowan, James, 81.
Rowan, Agnes, 83.
Rowan, Elizabeth, 83.
Rowan, Grizil, 83.
Rowan, Isabell, 83.
Rowan, James, 81.
Rowan, Jane, 100, 103.
Rowan, John, 58.
Rowan, Margaret, 83 (2).
Rowan, Mary, 83.
Rowan, Robert, 100, 102.

157

Schyner, Jacob, 60.
Schyner, Solomon, 60.
Scober, Maria Eliz'h, 62.
Scott, Agnes, 79.
Scott, Ann, 100.
Scott, David, 79.
Scott, Elizabeth, 79.
Scott, Grisil, 84.
Scott, Hannah, 83.
Scott, James, 82, 100.
Scott, Jane, 75, 79.
Scott, John, 75, 79, 84, 100, 123.
Scott, Margaret, 79.
Scott, Mary, 84, 100.
Scott, Richard, 75, 79.
Scott, Robert, 100.
Scott, Thomas, 125.
Scott, William, 100 (2), 102, 123, 126.
Scotland, 85.
Scruber, Andreas, 61.
Seawright, Andrew, 5.
Seawright, Elizabeth, 5, 6.
Seawright, George, 6.
Seawright, Helen, 6.
Seawright, James, 5.
Seawright, John, 6.
Seawright, Samuel, 6.
Seigle, Philip, 61.
Seigler, Margaret, 121.
Seiles, Johannes, 34.
Semour, Henry, 76.
Semple, John, 124.
Setzler, Ann(a) Christian, 61, 63.
Setzler, Ann Elizabeth, 63.
Setzler, Anna Maria, 63.
Setzler, Anna Marg't, 63.
Setzler, George Adam, 63.
Setzler, Johannes, 61.
Setzler, John Adam, 63.
Setzler, John George, 63.
Setzler, Peter, 61.
Sevitzer, George, 40.
Sevitzer, Margaret, 40.
Seveitzerin, Susanna Regina, 35, 41.
Seveitzenn, Regina, 35.
Seyfers, John, 56.
Seyferts, Anna Christian, 53.
Seyferts, Johannes, 53.
Seyferts, Silvanus, 53.
Seyler, Anne, 54.
Seyler, Christian, 54.
Seyler, David, 50.
Seyler, John, 50.
Shaffer, Michal, 41.
Shane, William, 127.
Shankley, William, 71.
Shanks, James, 70.
Shanks, Mathew, 67.

Shanks, William, 124.
Shanley, Thomas, 73.
Shannon, Samuel, 72.
Shannon, William, 66.
Sharpe, William (Englishman), 20.
Shauer, George, 41.
Shaw, John, 98, 99, 124.
Shawrer, Paul, 41.
Sheely, Catherine, 121.
Shelburne, Margaret, 66.
Sheild, Elizabeth, 123.
Sheildknight, Maria, 40.
Sheildknecter, Philip Jacob, 35.
Shelly, Mary, 121.
Shepherd, Mary, 124.
Sheralton, William, 66.
Sheriff Margaret, 33.
Sherin, Anna, 40.
Sherin, Uriah, 40.
Sherrer, Barbara, 38.
Sherrer, Michael, 41.
Sherrer, Urban, 38.
Sheuer, George, 36.
Sheurin, Catherine, 36.
Shewer, Johan, 38.
Shewrer, Magdalene, 38.
Shieldknight, Maria, 38.
Shieldknight, Rosina, 40.
Ships (see Boats).
Shoeber, Jacob, 35.
Shoemaker, Christian, 40.
Shoemaker, Christ'r Barbara, 121.
Shoemaker, Johannes, 38.
Shoemaker, Johan George, 35, 41.
Shoemaker, Margaret, 38.
Shorten, Eliz'h, 54.
Shorten, Johan Jacob, 54.
Shorten, Johannes, 54.
Shoulderin, John W., 54.
Shoulderin, Maria, 54.
Shulles, Henry Abraham, 127.
Shurrs, Michael, 15.
Simmons, Jeremiah, 86.
Simms, Edward, 80 (see Sminns also).
Simpson, Andrew, 87, 91, 119.
Simpson, Hugh, 47.
Simpson, James, 33.
Simpson, Jane, 120.
Simpson, John, 120.
Simpson, Robert, 120.
Simpson, William, 120.
Simpton, John, 100.
Simpton, Margaret, 99.
Simpton, Mary, 99.
Simpton, Robert, 99, 102.
Simpton, Sarah, 99.
Sims, John, 68.
Simson, James, 65.

160

Timble, Henry, 42.
Tisdale, James, 12.
Tisdale, Jane, 12.
Tisdale, Margaret, 12.
Toad, Marg't, 123.
Toad, Robert, 123.
Todd, Archibald, 125.
Todd, Jean, 126.
Todd, William, 86.
Tomanick, Mary, 121.
Tomb, Alexander, 99, 102.
Tomb, David, 99.
Tomb, Elizabeth, 99.
Torrans, Pouag & Co., 47, 48, 49, 68, 70, 76, 80, 84, 91, 95, 98, 102, 104, 108.
Torrens, Greg & Pouag, 9.
Towbert, George, 127.
Townsend, Ezekiel, 107.
Townshend, Ezekiel, 103.
Trein, Michael Greissen, 35.
Tufts, James, 119.
Turk, Ann, 77.
Turk, Jane, 77.
Turk, Jannett, 74, 77.
Turk, John, 74, 77.
Turk, William, 74, 77.
Turner, Alexander, 101, 102.
Turner, James, 101, 107, 109.
Turner, John, 101, 102.
Turner, Joseph, 47.
Turner, Margaret, 101.
Turner, Susannah, 109 (2).
Turner, Thomas, 68.
Turner, William, 101, 102.
Tweed, Eleanor, 123.
Tweed, James, 122, 123.

U

Underbrank, Anna Maria, 53.
Underbrank, John, 53.
Unsman, Andreas, 38.
Ursman, Christopher, 38.
Urwin, Dorothy, 28.
Urwin, Henry, 28.
Usher, Ann, 88 (2).
Usher, Daniel, 88.
Usher, David, 88 (2), 91.
Usher, John, 88, 91.
Uts, Diedrick, 61.
Uts, Eva Catherine, 63.
Uts, George Peter, 63.
Uts, Maria Catherine, 63.
Utsin, Anna Margaret, 61.

V

Vallae, Jacque, 22.
Varner, James, 123.
Vernon, Alexander, 71.
Vernon, Robert, 92, 93.
Vernor, Jane, 78.
Vernor, John, 75, 78.
Vernor, Martha, 78.
Vernor, Mary, 78.
Vernor, Robert, 78.
Viddle, Mary, 121.
Villerett, Louis, 21.
Vittle, Marg't Eliz'th, 121.
Voice, Jane, 86.
Volhill, Ann Marg't, 64.
Voltrall, Jacob, 60.

W

Wadmeller, Johan Fred'k, 41.
Waggener, Manerwell, 42.
Waid, Joseph, 108, 110.
Waight, Benjamin, 107.
Waight, John, 103 (2), 107 (2).
Waight, Mary, 107.
Waight, Samuel, 103, 107.
Waight, Sarah, 103, 107.
Waite, Eleanor, 106.
Waite, John, 104, 106.
Waite, Mary, 106.
Walk, Anna Catherine, 38.
Walk, John Conrad, 38.
Walk, Martin, 38.
Walker, Agnes, 47, 84 (2), 125.
Walker, Andrew, 90.
Walker, Elizabeth, 84, 90.
Walker, Francis, 82.
Walker, Isabella, 82.
Walker, Isobell, 84.
Walker, James, 82.
Walker, Jane, 90.
Walker, Jannet, 48.
Walker, John, 47, 48, 82, 84, 90, 92, 97, 98, 118.
Walker, John, Jun'r, 82.
Walker, Joseph, 46.
Walker, Margaret, 84 (2).
Walker, Martha, 48.
Walker, Mary, 84 (3), 90.
Walker, Robert, 32, 122.
Walker, Samuel, 48.
Walker, Thomas, 48, 90.
Walker, William, 82.
Walla, Joseph, 54.
Walla, Maria, 54.
Wallace, Agnes, 101.
Wallace, Eleanor, 105.
Wallace, Elizabeth, 101, 103, 105.

Wylie, Francis, 89, 92.
Wylie, Henry, 95, 96.
Wylie, James, 88, 89, 91, 92.
Wylie, Jane, 95 (2), 96.
Wylie, John, 88.
Wylie, Margaret, 88, 89, 92, 95.
Wylie, Mary, 89.
Wylie, Peter, 89, 92.
Wylie, Rebecca, 88.
Wylie, Robert, 89, 92.
Wylie, Samuel, 88.
Wylie, Sarah, 88.
Wylie, Thomas, 95 (2), 96 (2).
Wylie, William, 89, 90, 92.
Wyly, John, 118.
Wynberger, Anna Catherine, 63 (2).
Wynberger, Anna Rosina, 63.
Wynberger, Eva Catherine, 63.
Wynberger, John George, 63.

Y

Yan, George Adam, 61. 6
Yeason, Ann Dorothea Elizabeth, 112.
Youart, Andrew, 67 (2).
Youart, Elizabeth, 69.
Youart, James, 67.
Yourat, Mary, 69 (2).
Youart, Rachel, 69.
Youart, Samuel, 69.
Young, Agnes, 100, 120.
Young, Agness, 80.
Young, Andrew, 123.
Young, Ann, 125.
Young, Elizabeth, 68, 100.
Young, Henrick, 61.
Young, Henry, 120.
Young, Hugh, 100, 102.
Young, Isabel, 123.
Young, James, 100, 124.
Young, Jane, 76, 80, 100, 102.
Young, Janet, 123.
Young, Jannett, 69.
Young, Jean, 126.
Young, Johannes Nicholas, 61.
Young, John, 68, 76, 80.
Young, Margaret, 100.
Young, Mary, 80, 123.
Young, Matthew, 120.
Young, Robert, 68, 76, 80.
Young, Samuel, 9, 68, 69, 100, 102.

Young, Sarah, 100, 102.
Young, William, 123, 125.

Z

Zang, Christian, 34, 36, 39.
Zang, John, 39.
Zang, John Jacob, 39.
Zang, John Peter, 39.
Zang, Juliana, 36.
Zanss, Johannes, 34.
Zants, Johanes, 37.
Zebberdeen, Marg't, 37.
Zehman, Dorothea, 40.
Zehman, Henry, 40.
Zehuder, George Philip, 60.
Zeiserin, Catherine, 40.
Zemferin, Madelina, 35.
Zemmerman, Frederick, 35.
Zemmerman, Philip, 34.
Zentzen, Andreas, 41.
Zetheman, Eva, 39.
Zeusevin, Magdelen, 41.
Zimmeral, Anna Marg'ta, 63.
Zimmeral, Anna Maria, 63.
Zimmeral, Johannes, 63.
Zimmeral, Johannes Adam, 63.
Zimmeral, Maria Catherine, 63.
Zimmeral, Maria Eliz'th, 63.
Zimmerle, Anna, 62.
Zimmerle, Anna Marg't, 61.
Zimmerle, Grassanha, 62.
Zimmerle, Hans, 61.
Zimmerle, John Philip, 61.
Zimmerle, John Jacob, 61.
Zimmerle, Mary Eliz'h, 61.
Zimmerman, Adalalia, 39.
Zimmerman, Anna, 39 (2).
Zimmerman, Apolonia, 36.
Zimmerman, Frederick, 37.
Zimmerman, George, 40.
Zimmerman, Jacob, 62.
Zimmerman, Johannes, 39.
Zimmerman, Margaret, 37.
Zimmerman, Peter, 39.
Zimmerman, Philip, 36.
Zinman, Elizabeth, 37.
Zinman, Michael, 37.
Zwertzer, Christian, 38.
Zwilling, George, 39.
Zwilling, Johannes, 35, 39.
Zwilling, Maria, 36.

CPSIA information can be obtained at www.ICGtesting.com
Printed in the USA
BVOW04s2118310315

394156BV00007B/70/P